I0422474

Lovely Flowers

Coloring Book for Adults

Avri Maplewood

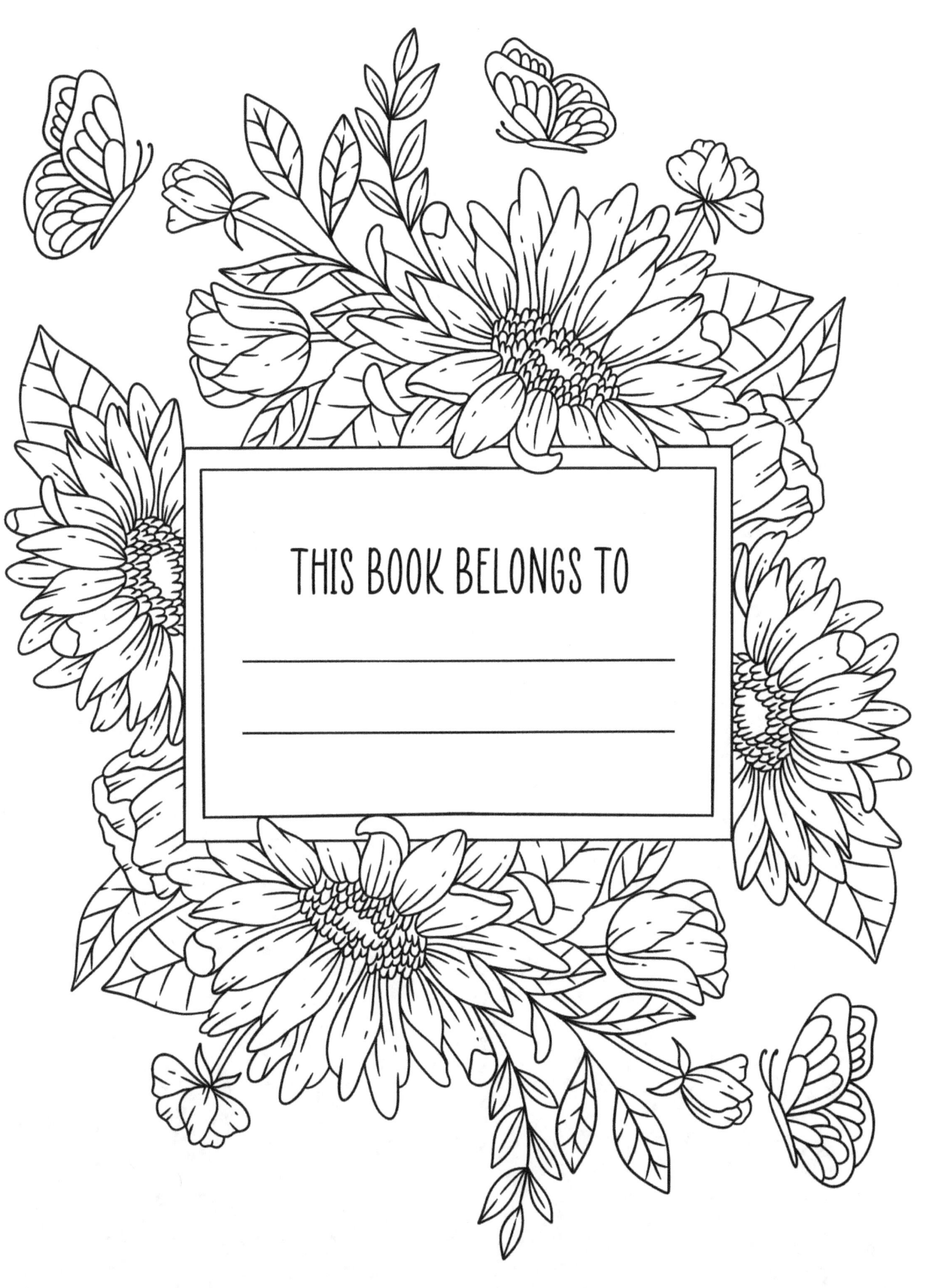

THIS BOOK BELONGS TO

_____

_____

TABLE OF CONTENTS (1 OF 2)

TABLE OF CONTENTS (2 OF 2)

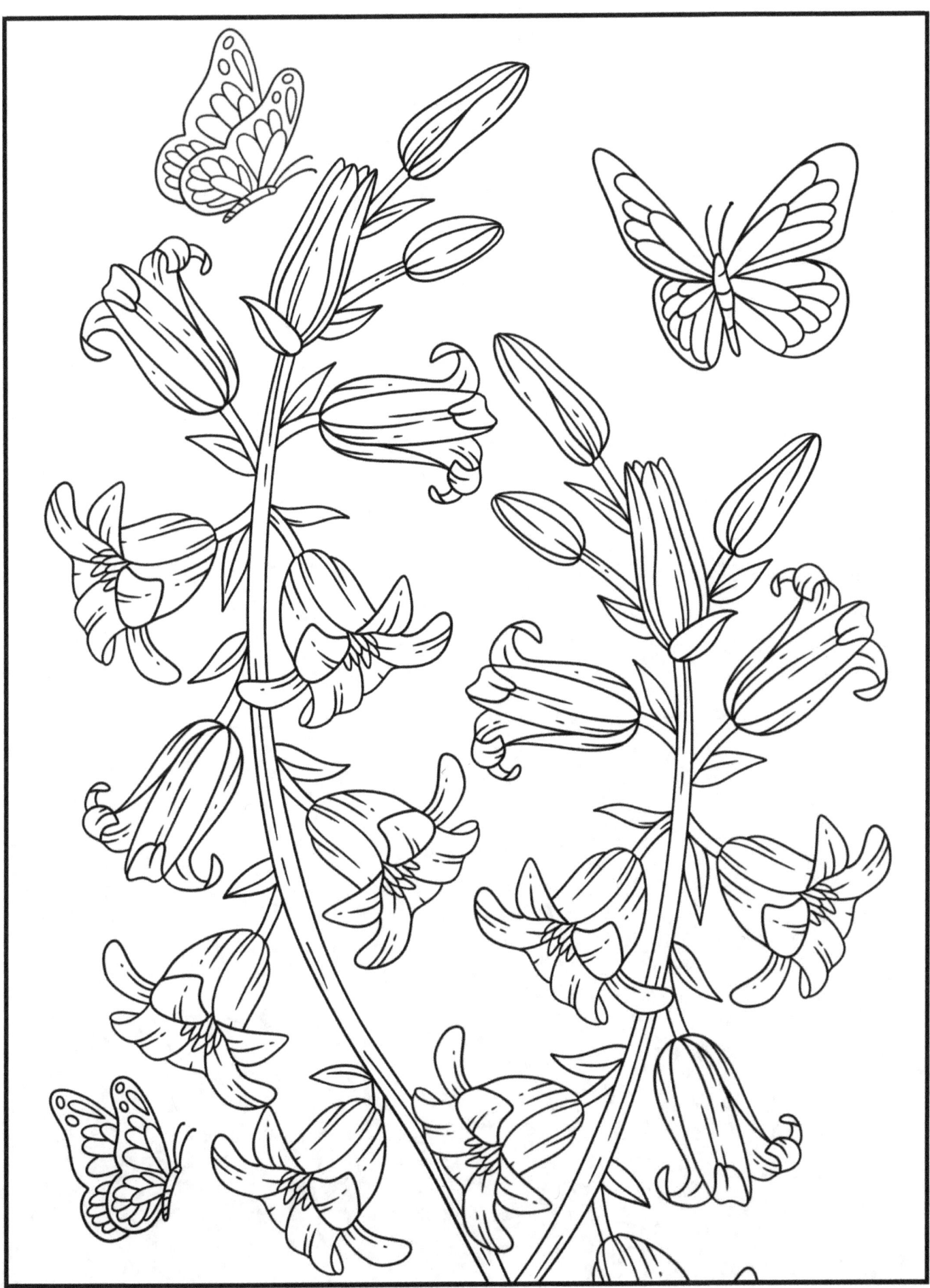

9

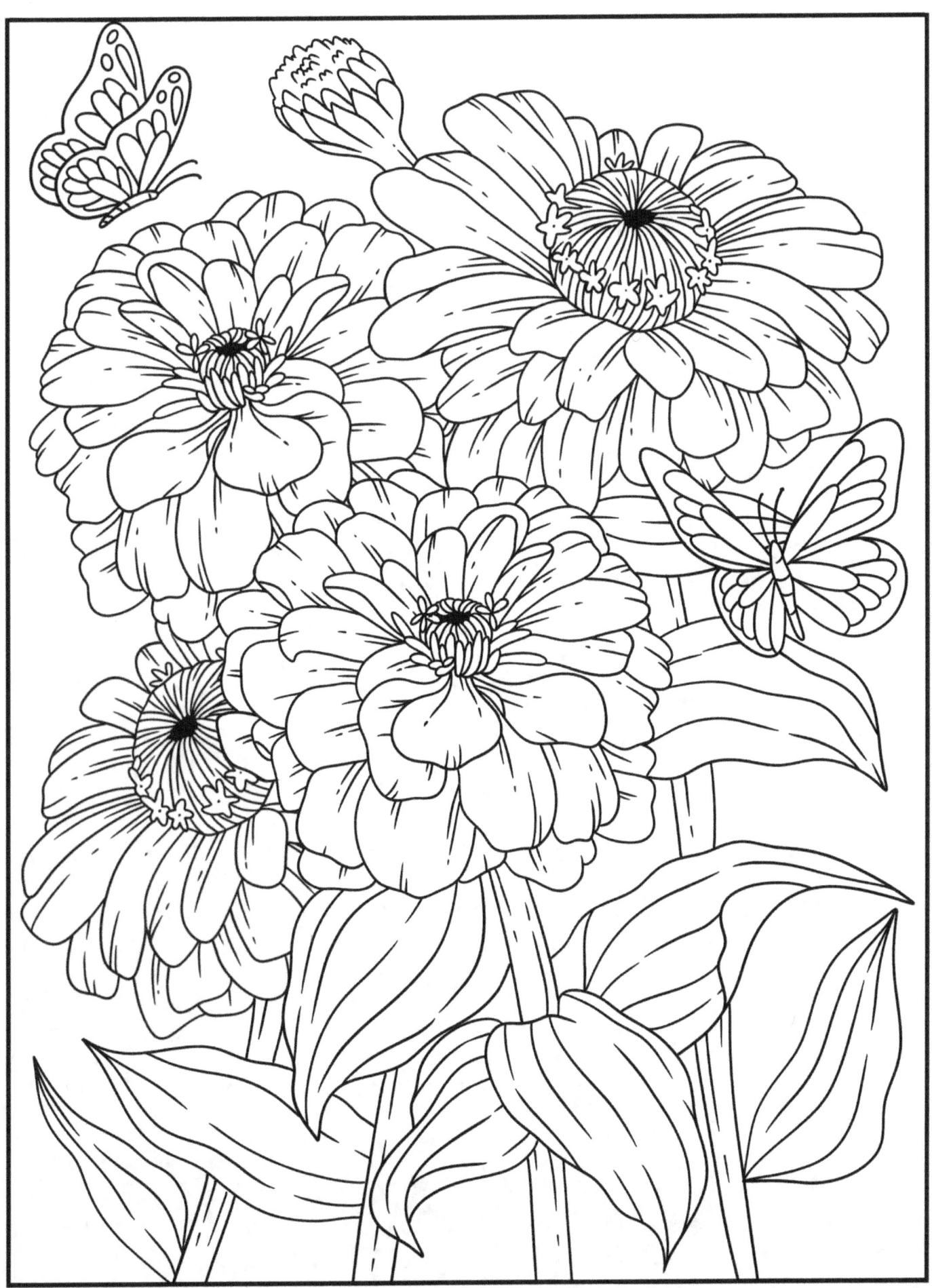

11

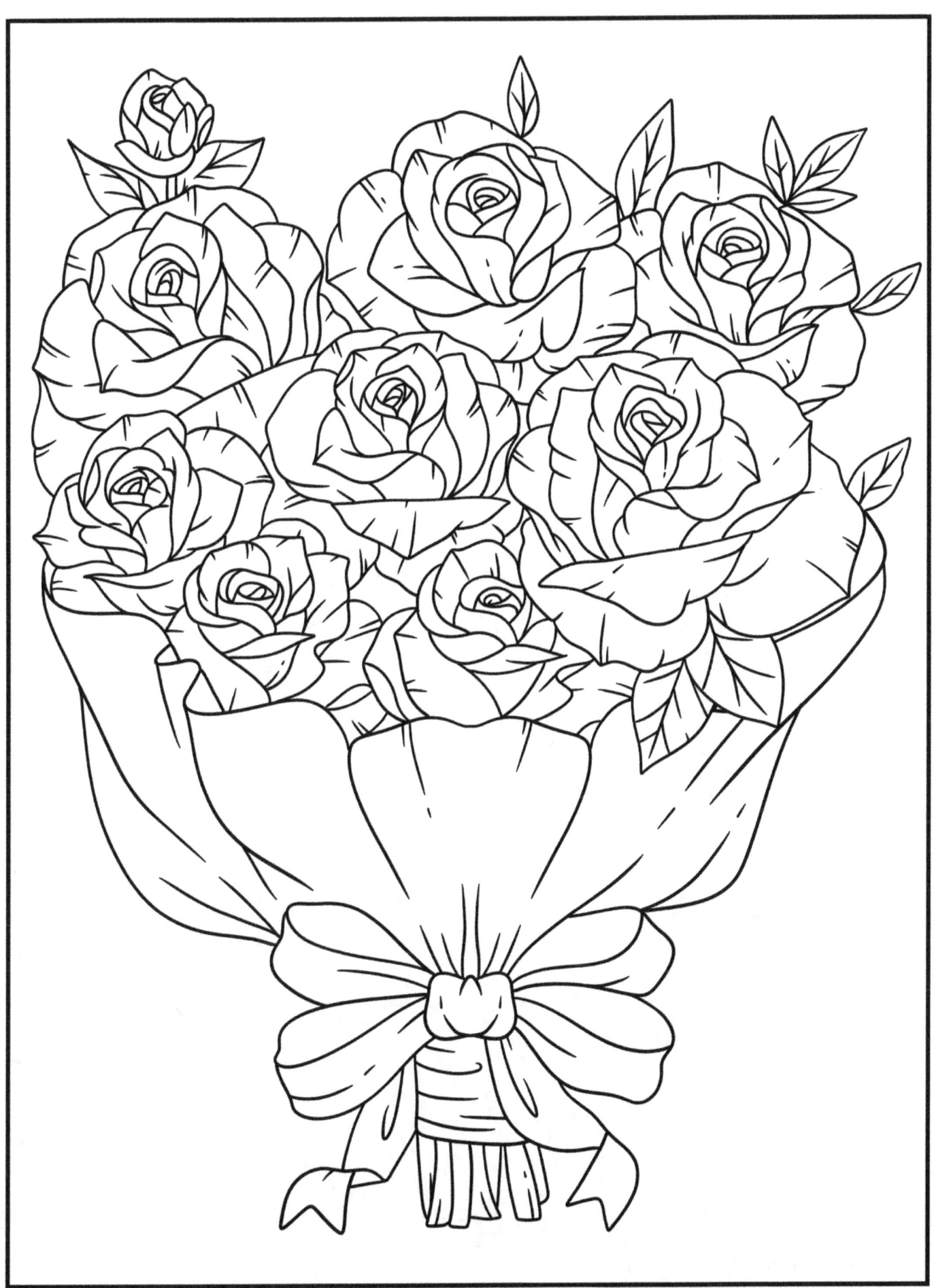

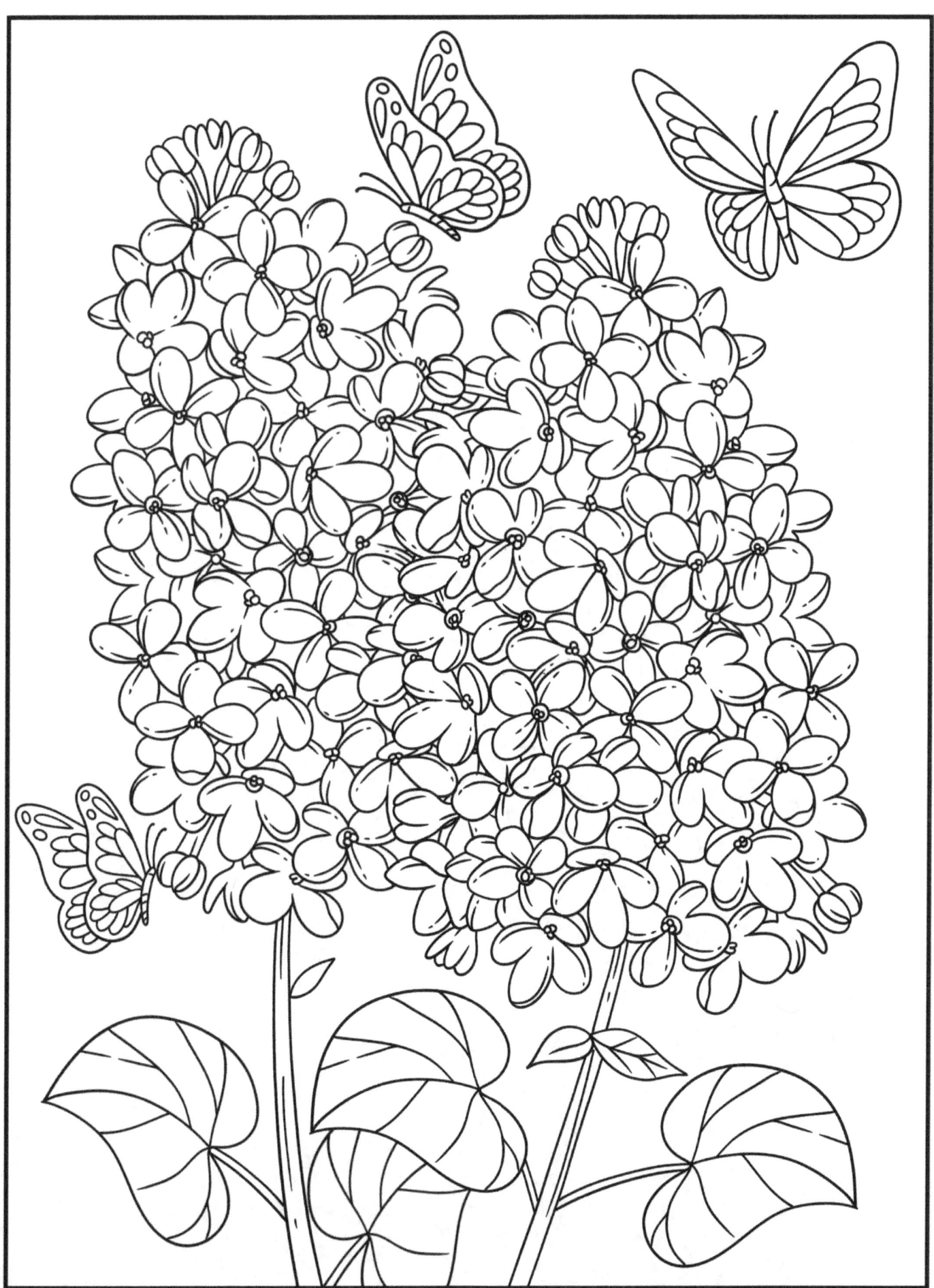

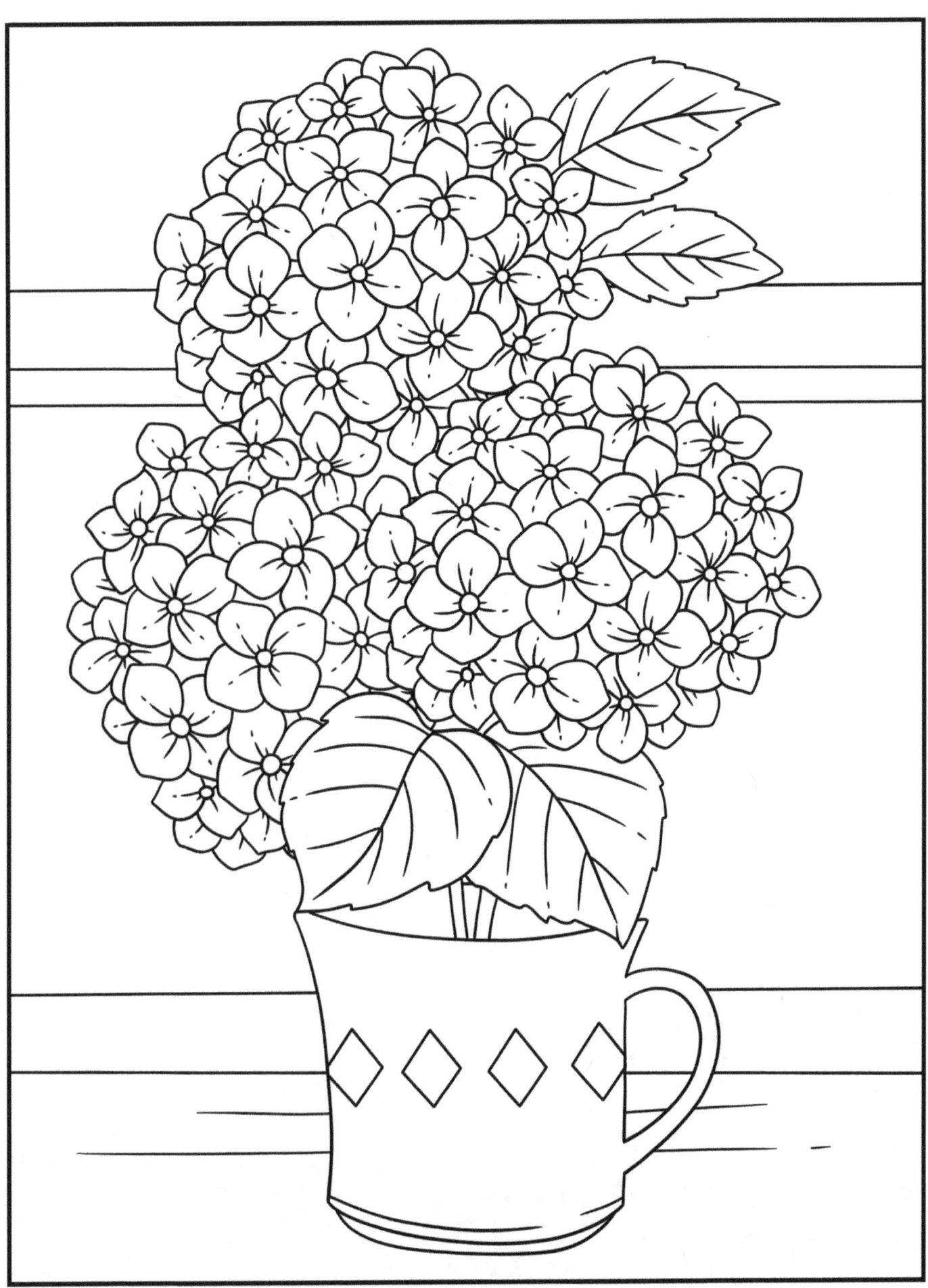

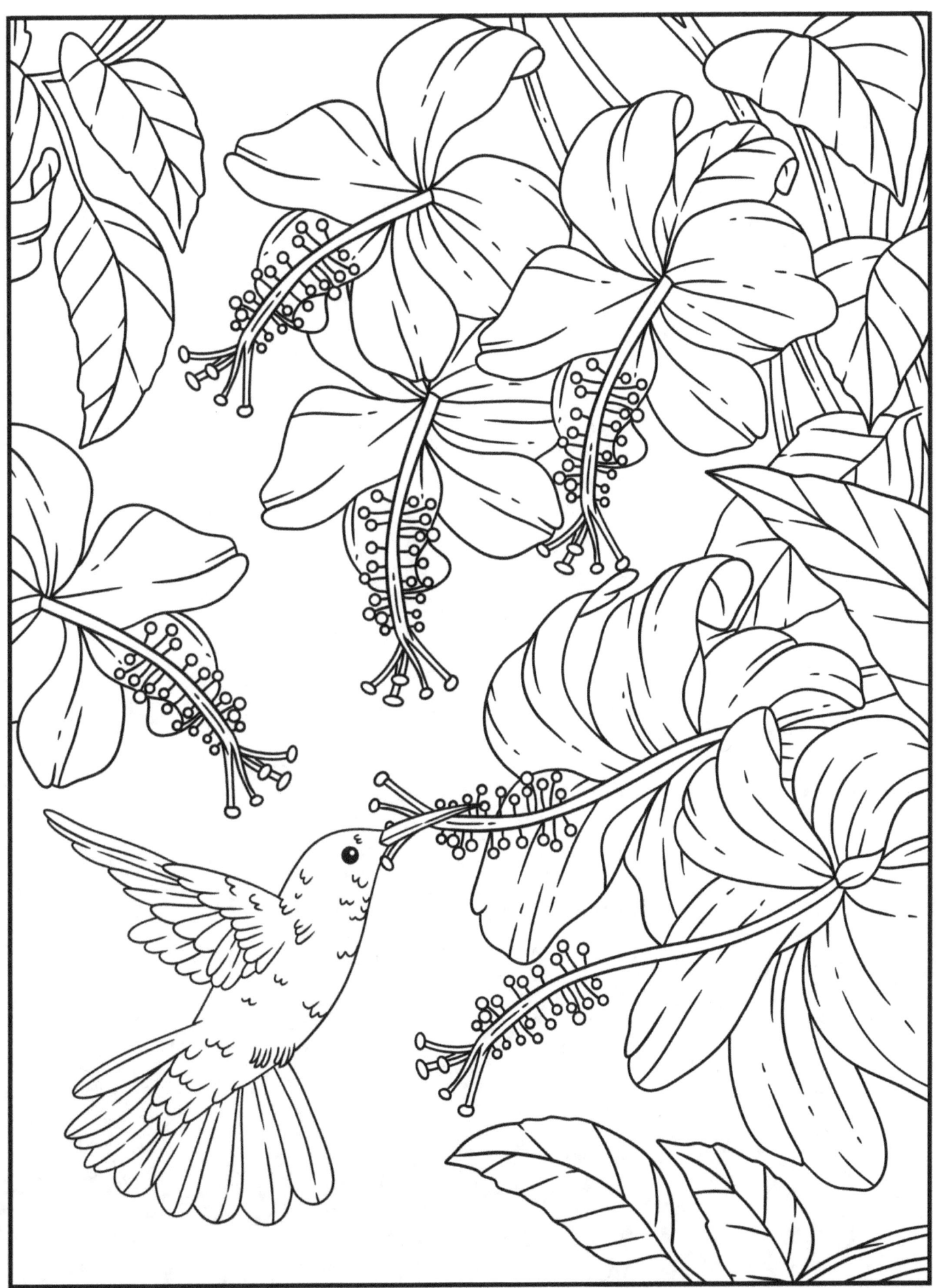

19

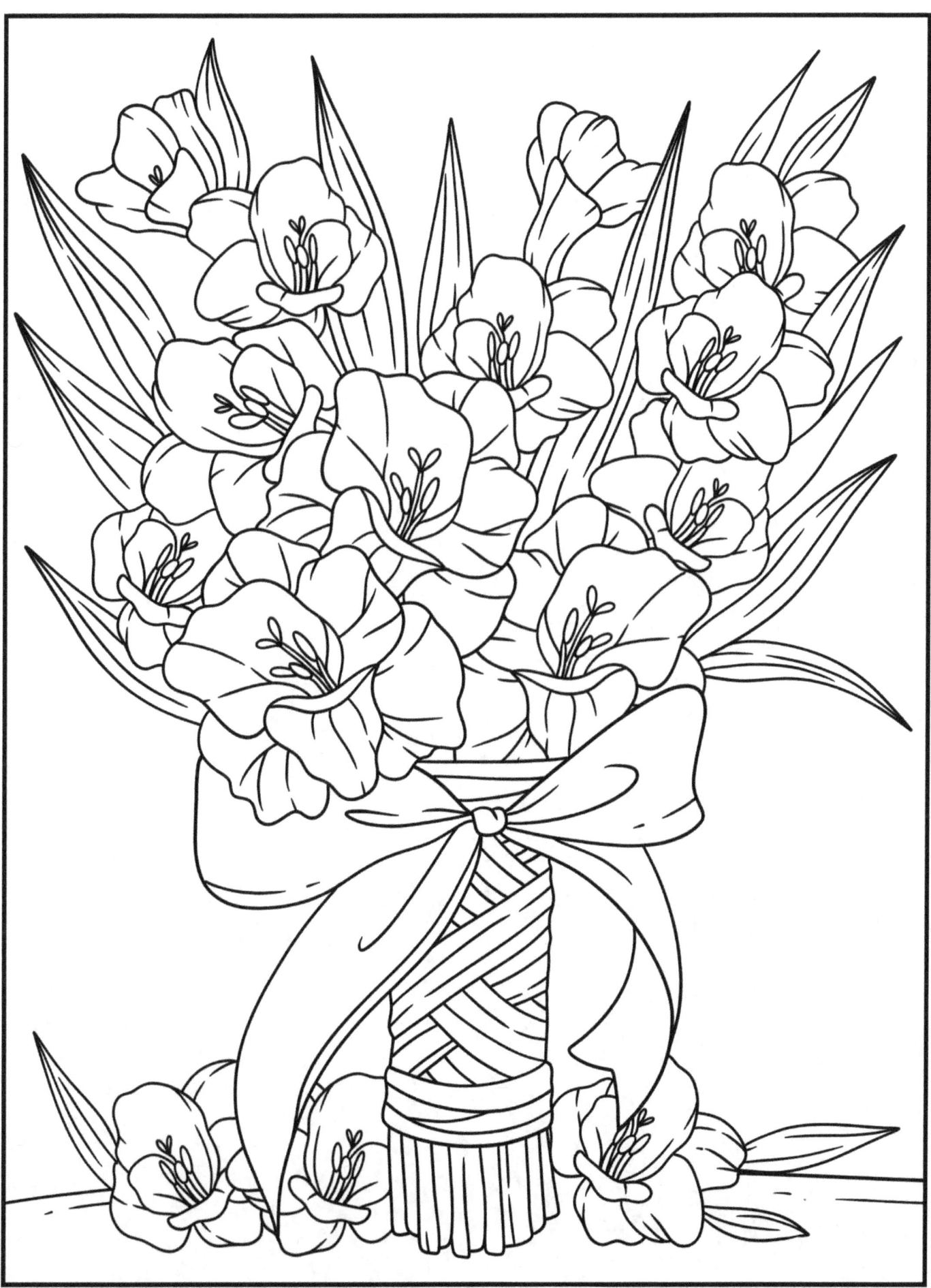

21

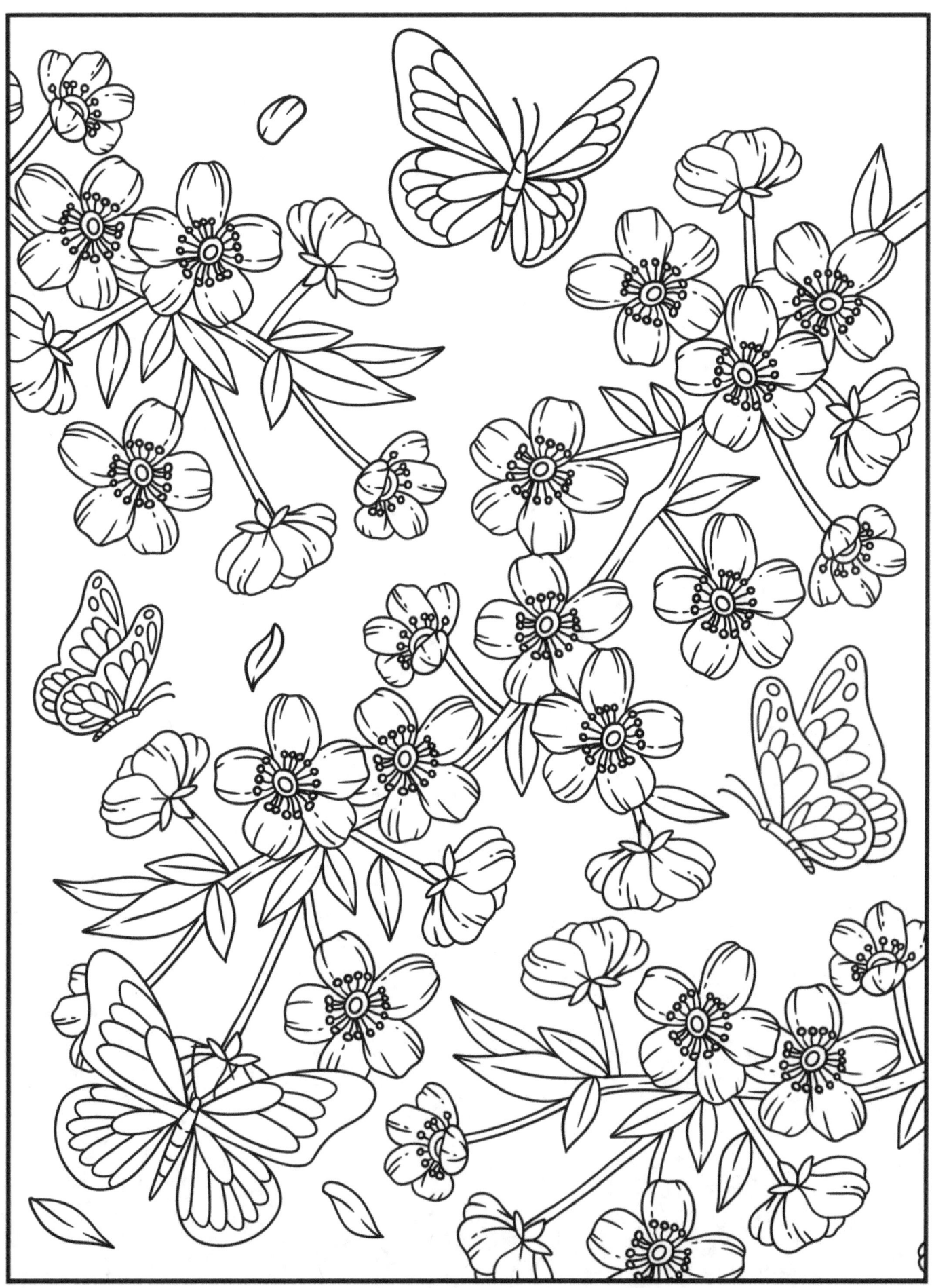

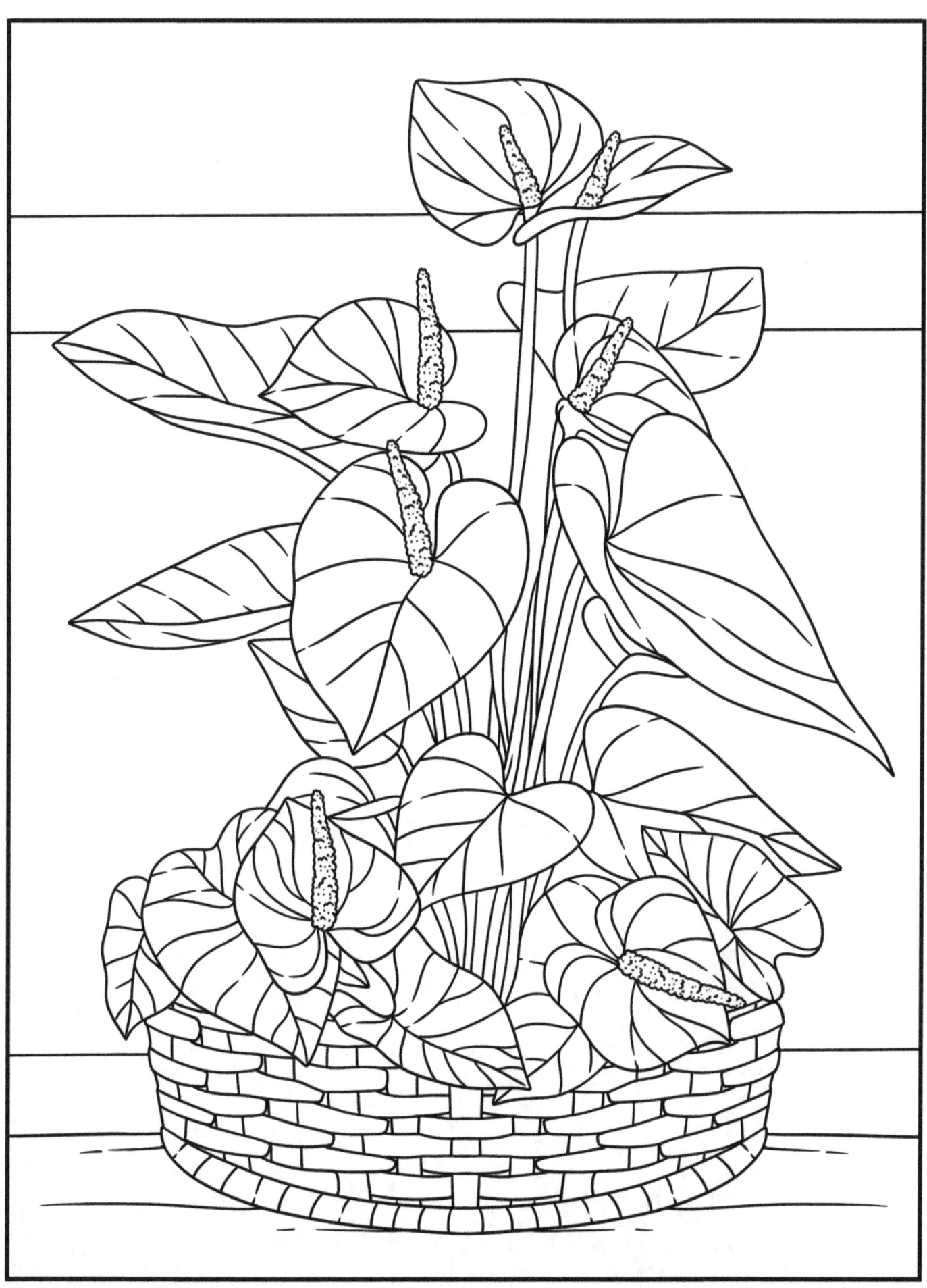

25

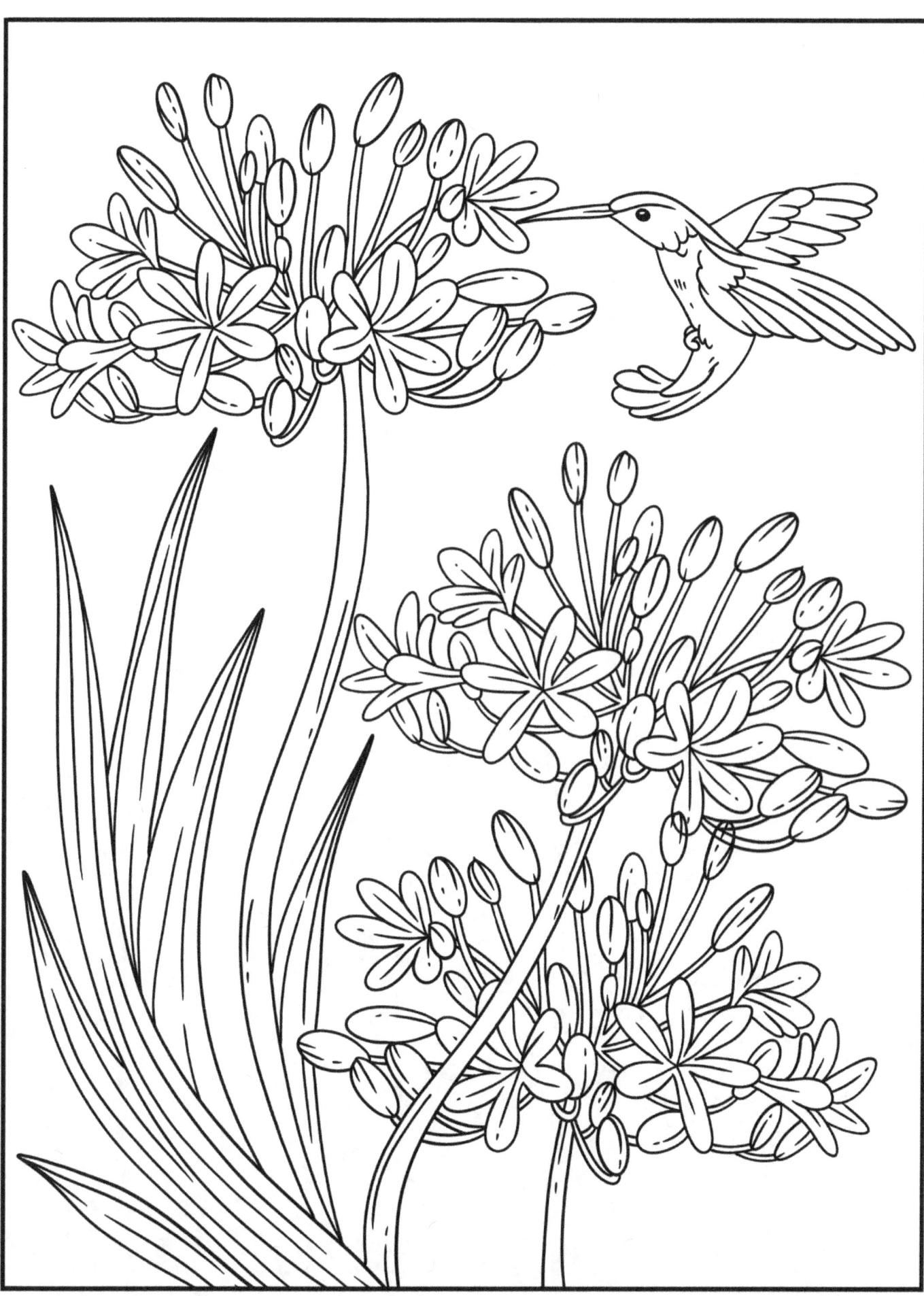

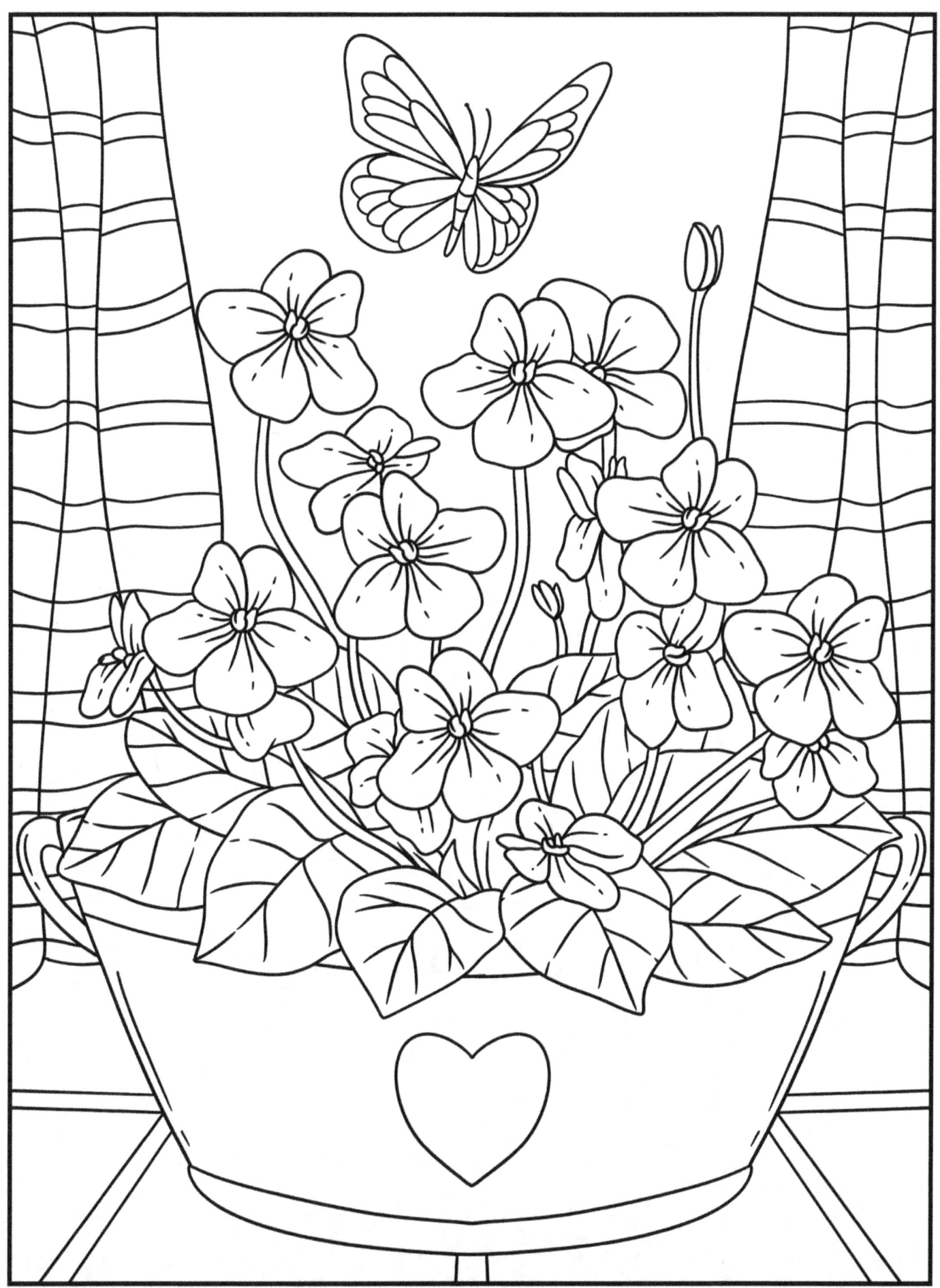

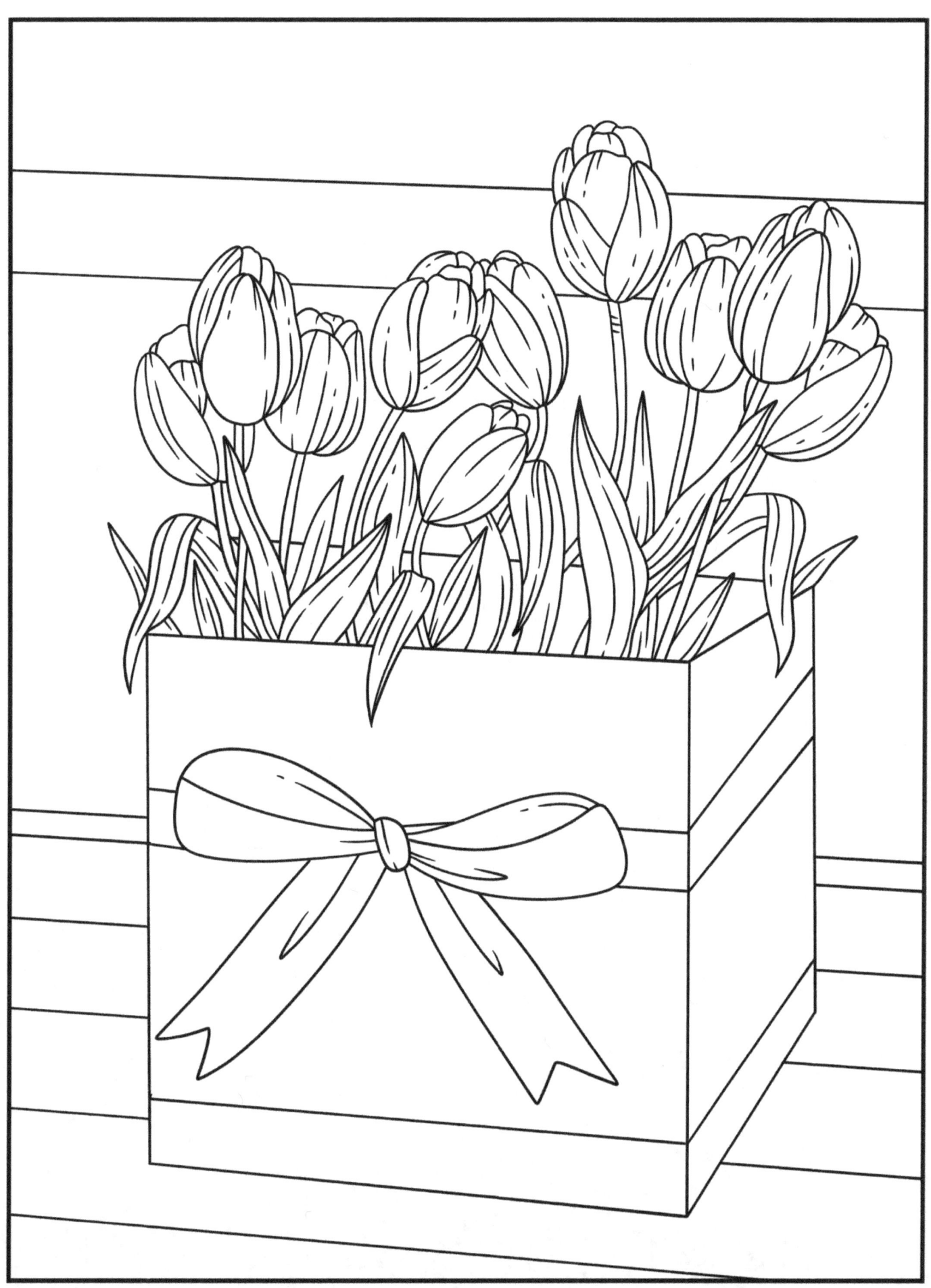

31

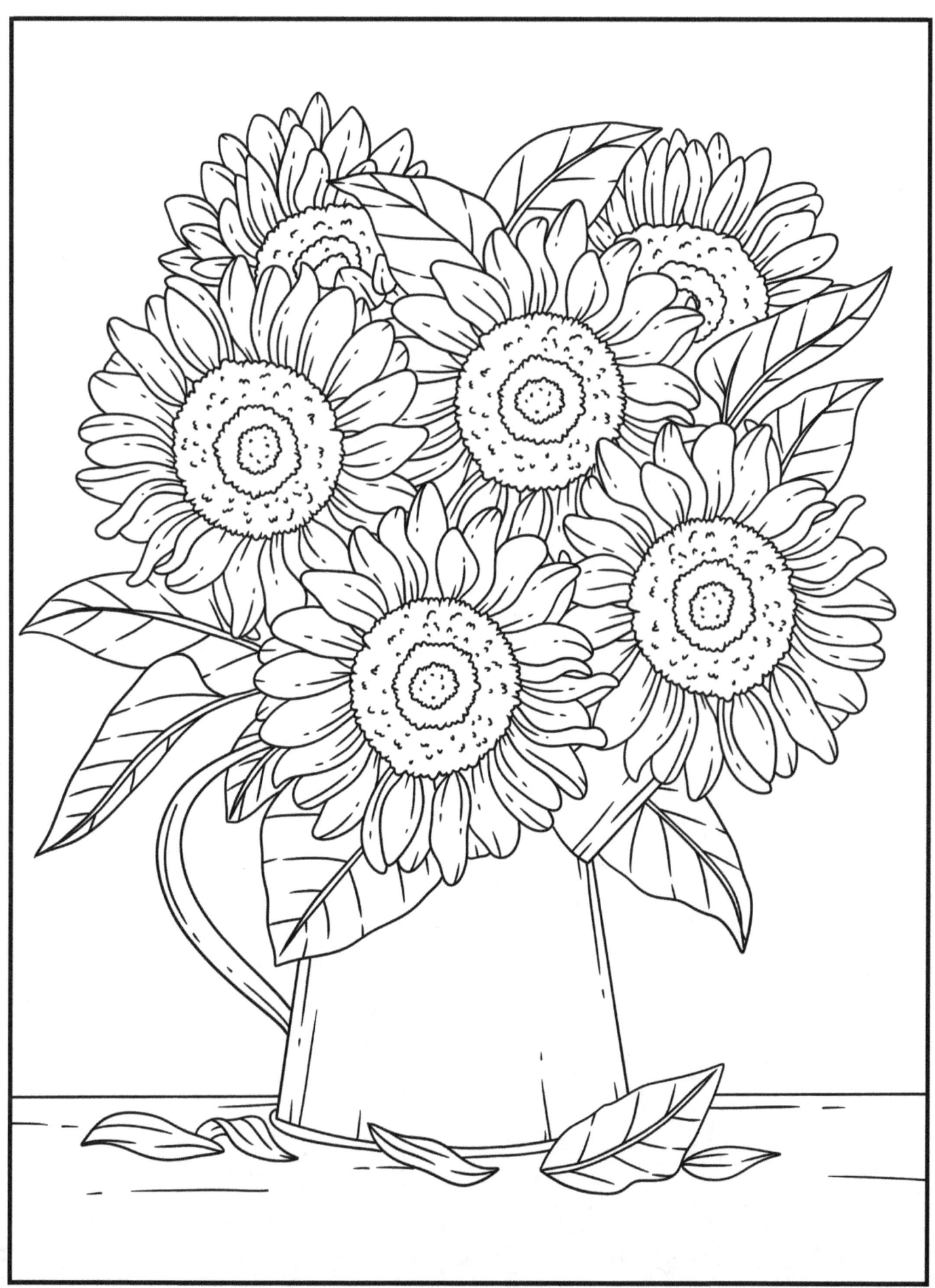

33

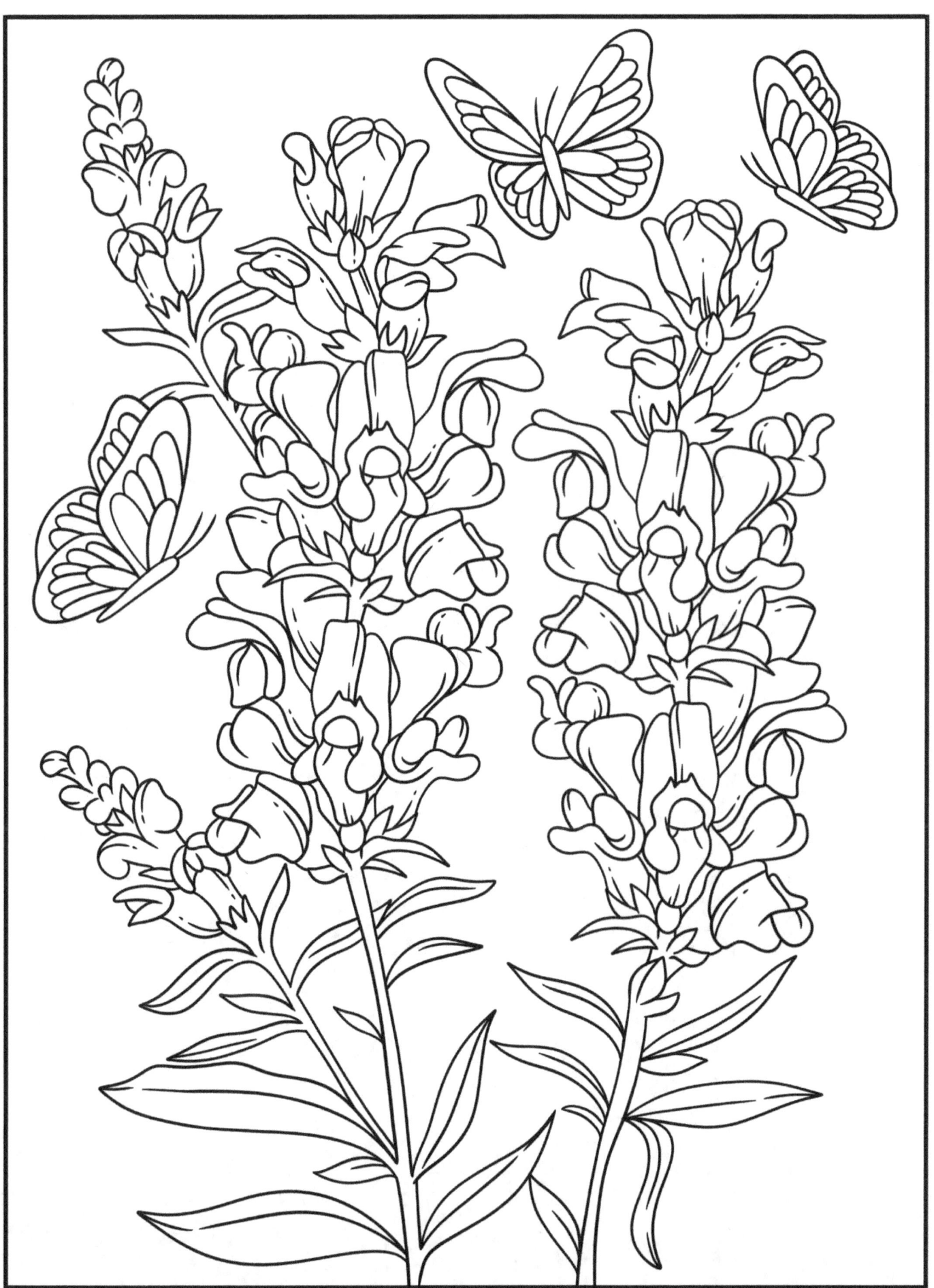

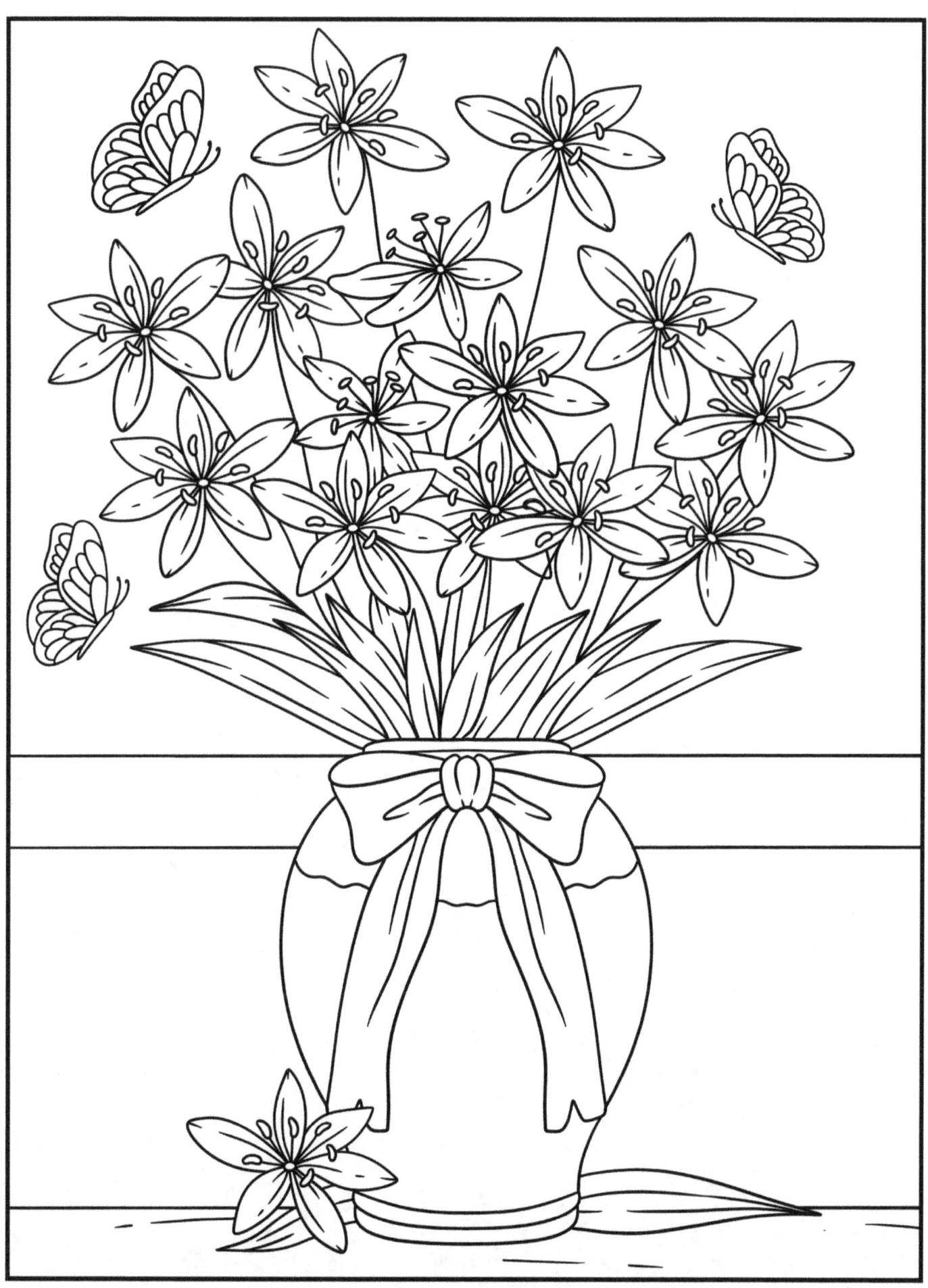

37

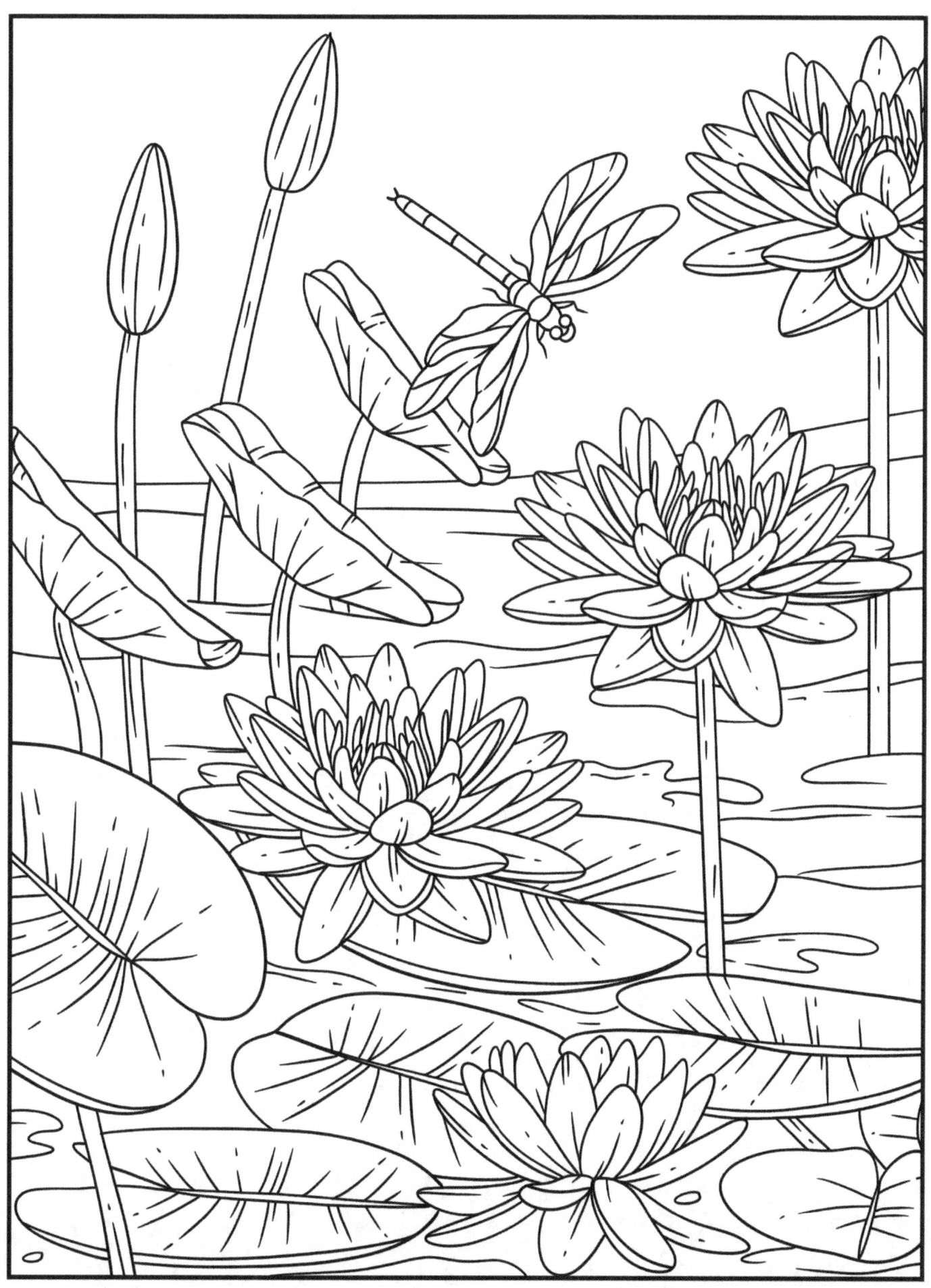

39

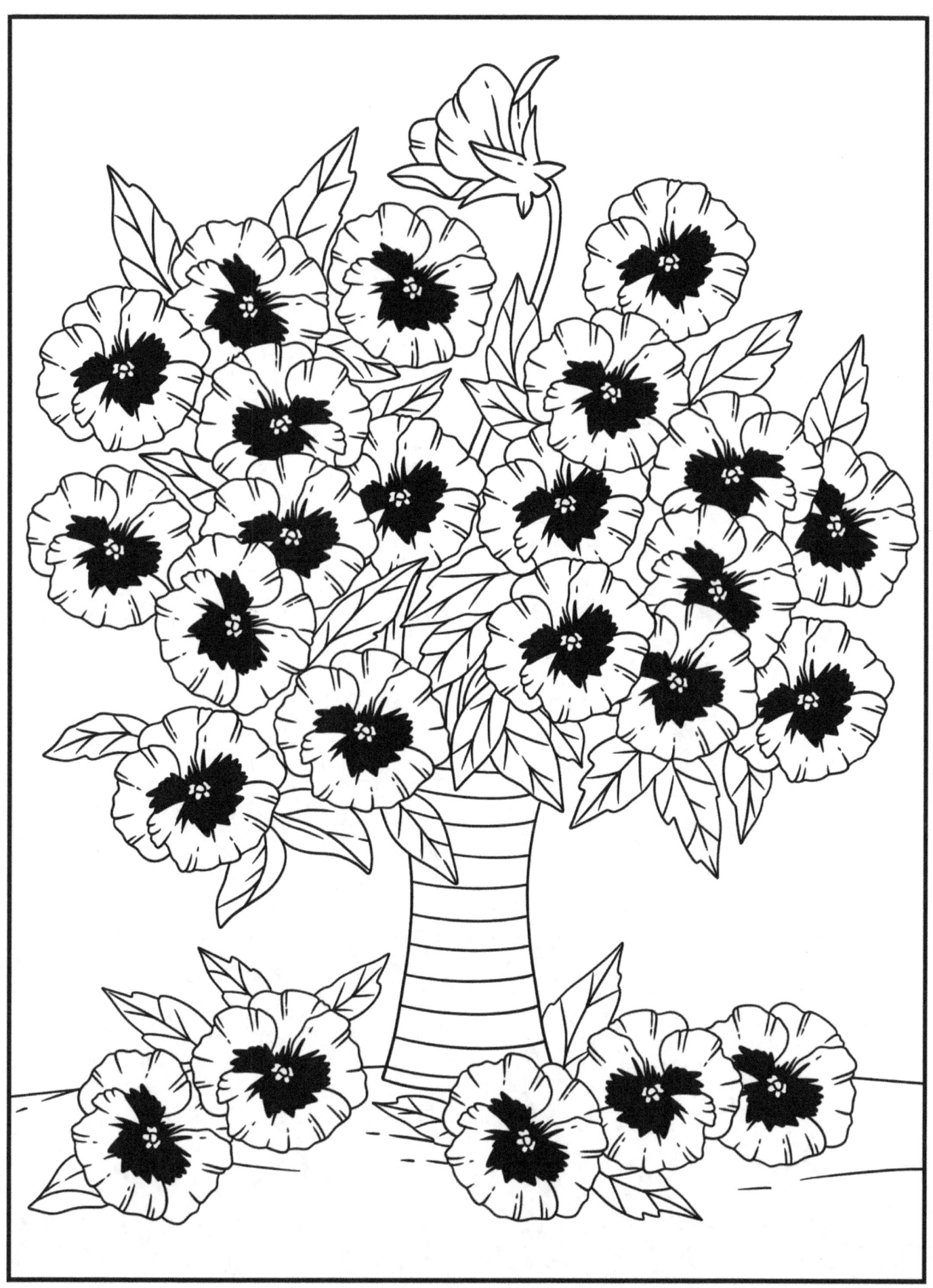

41

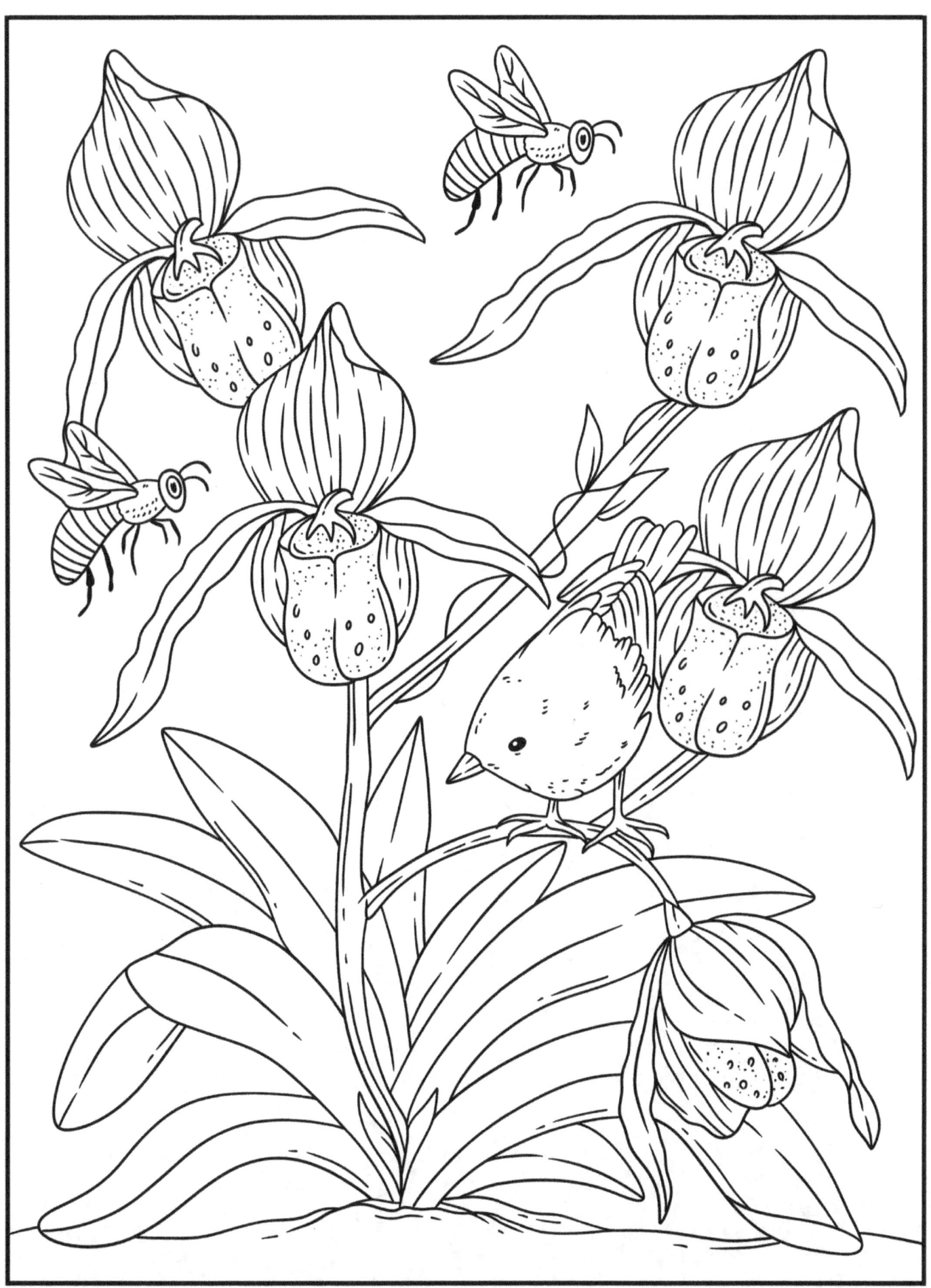

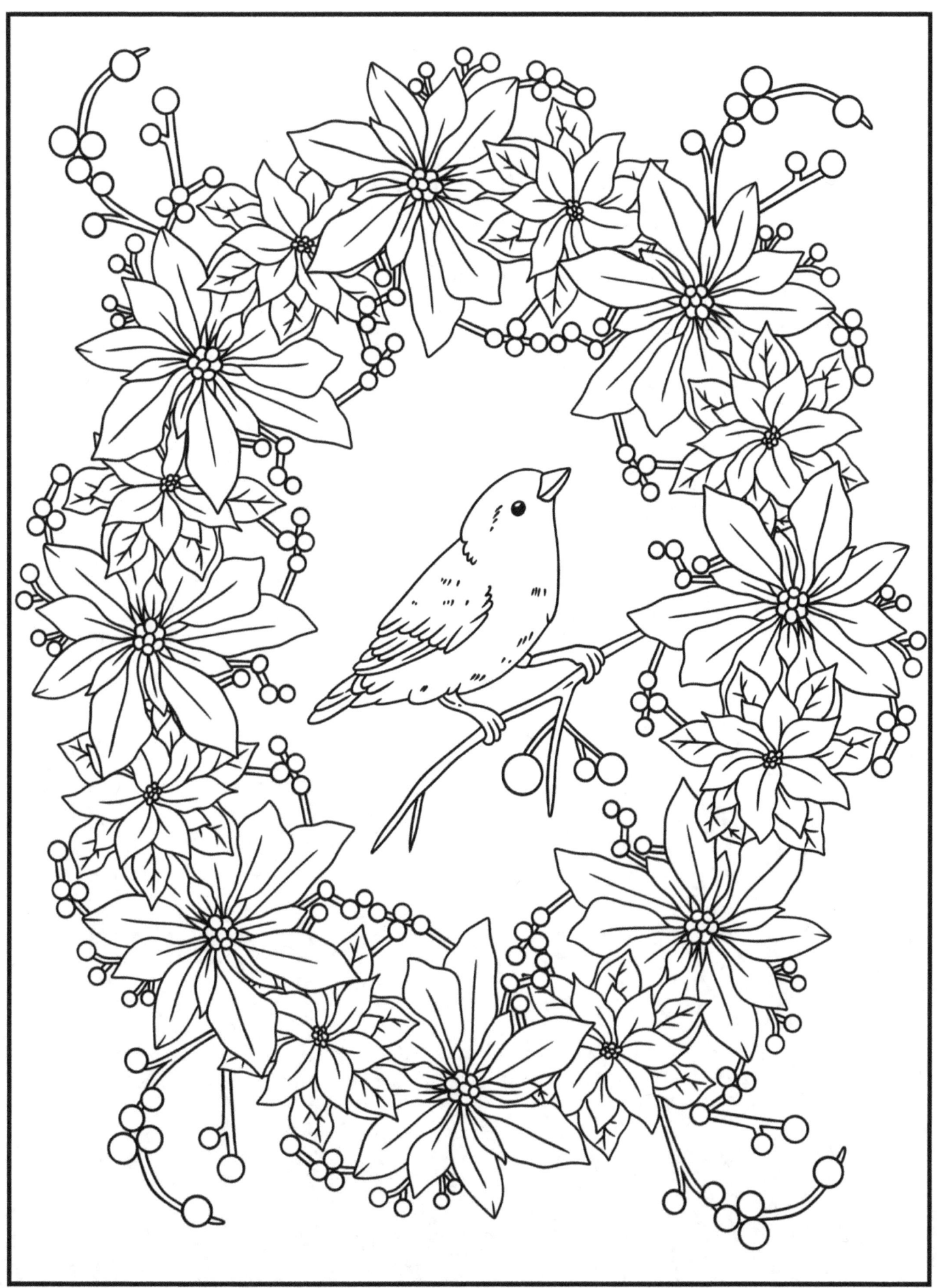

45

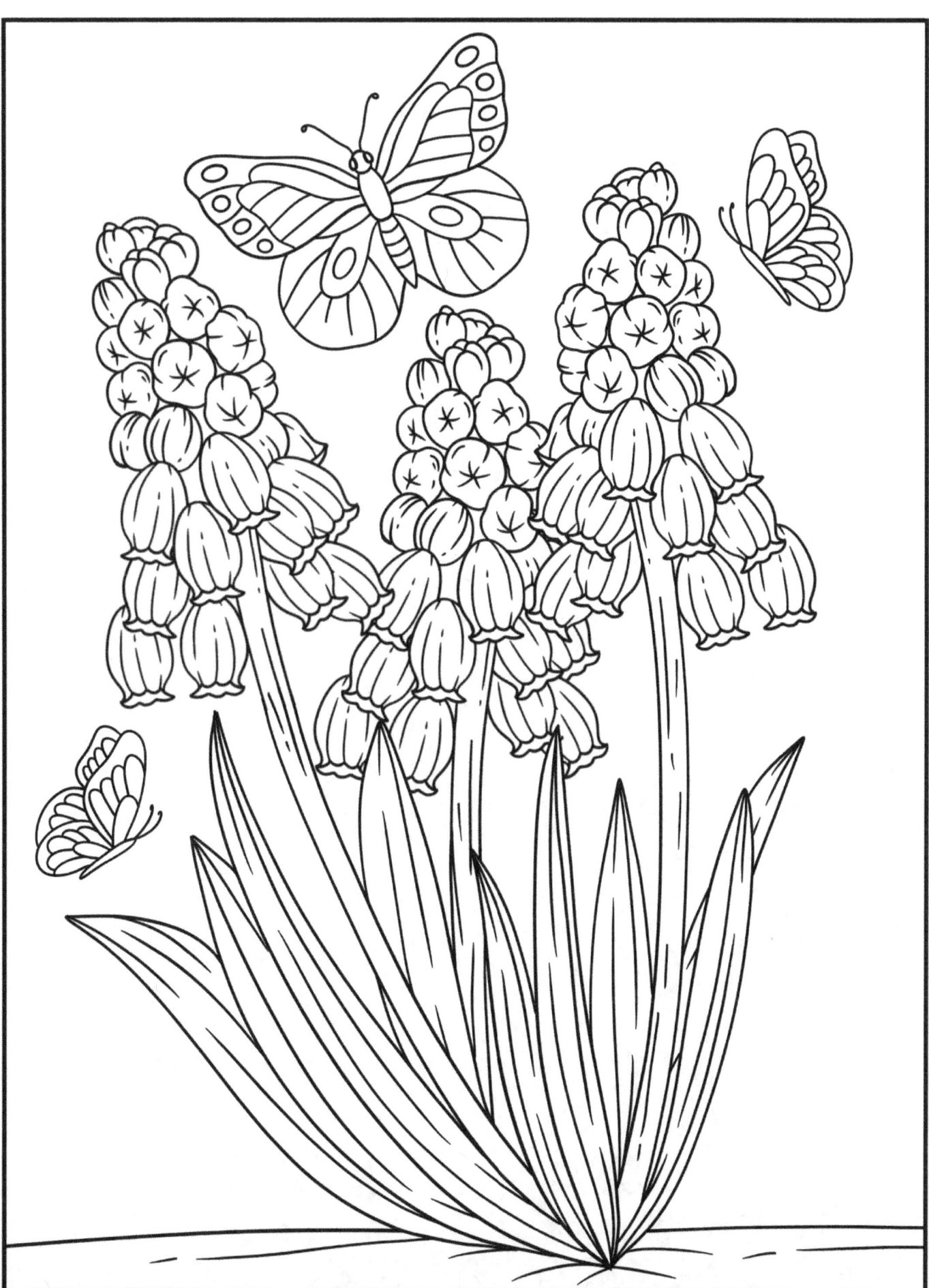

47

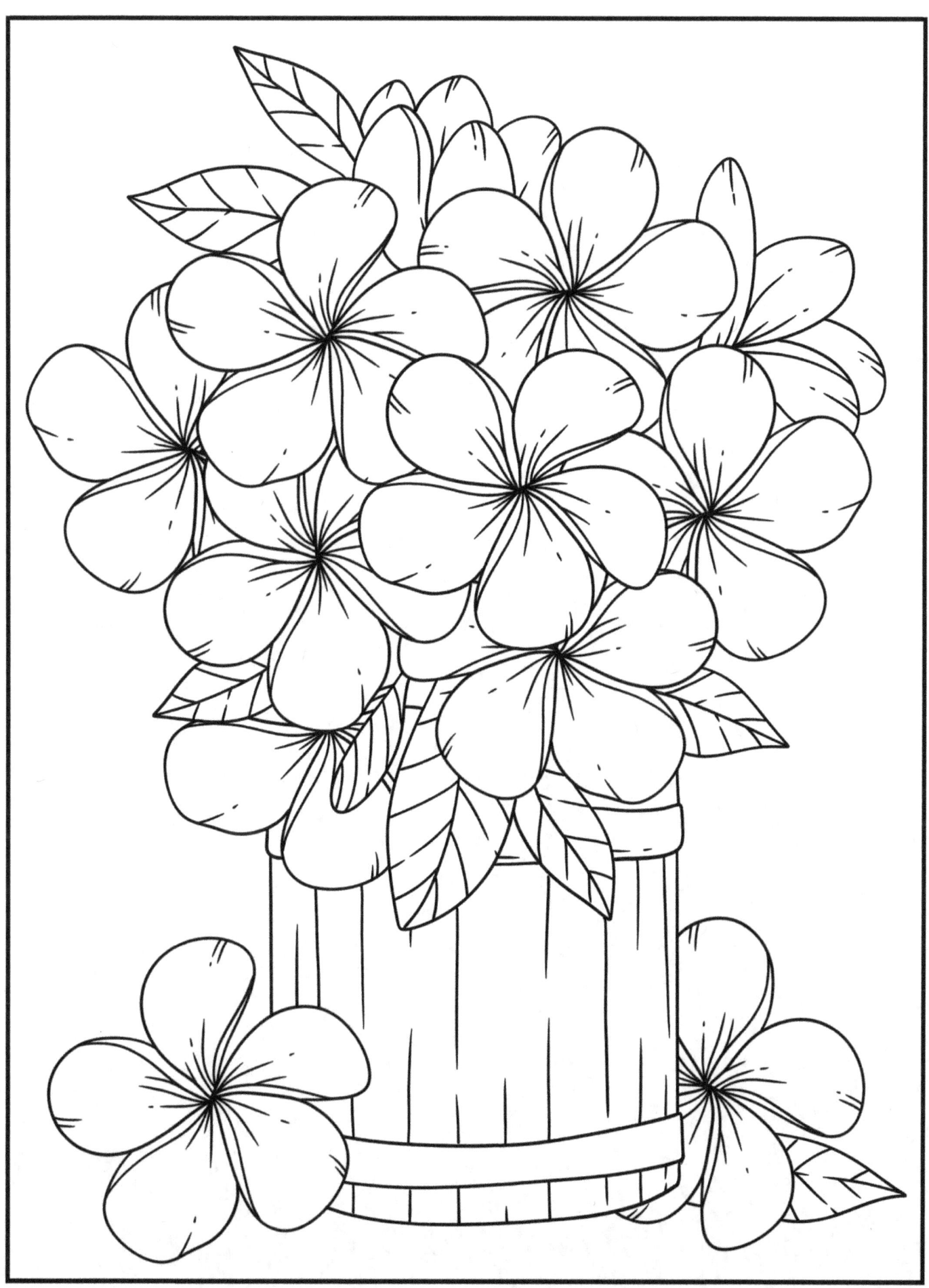

49

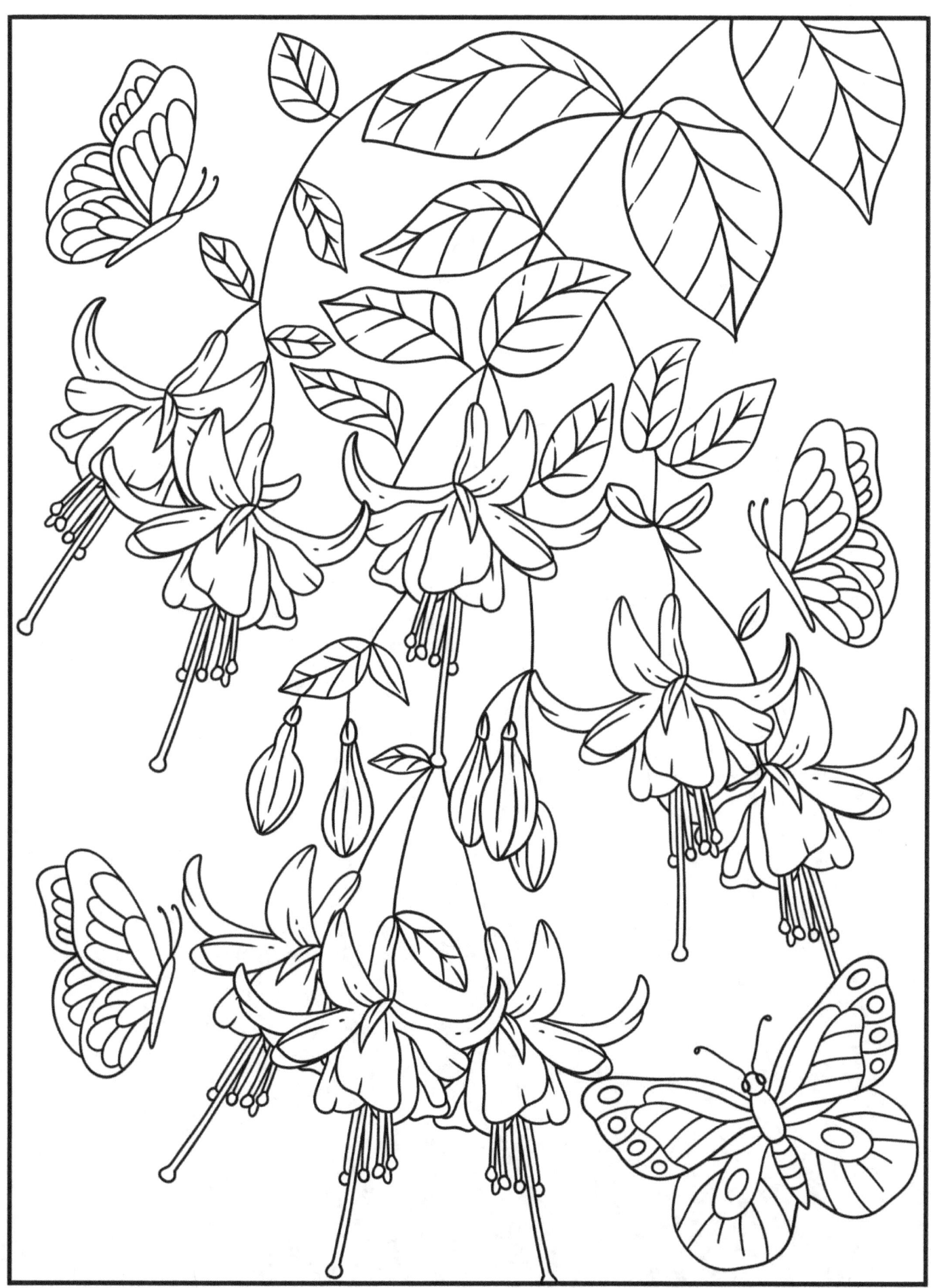

51

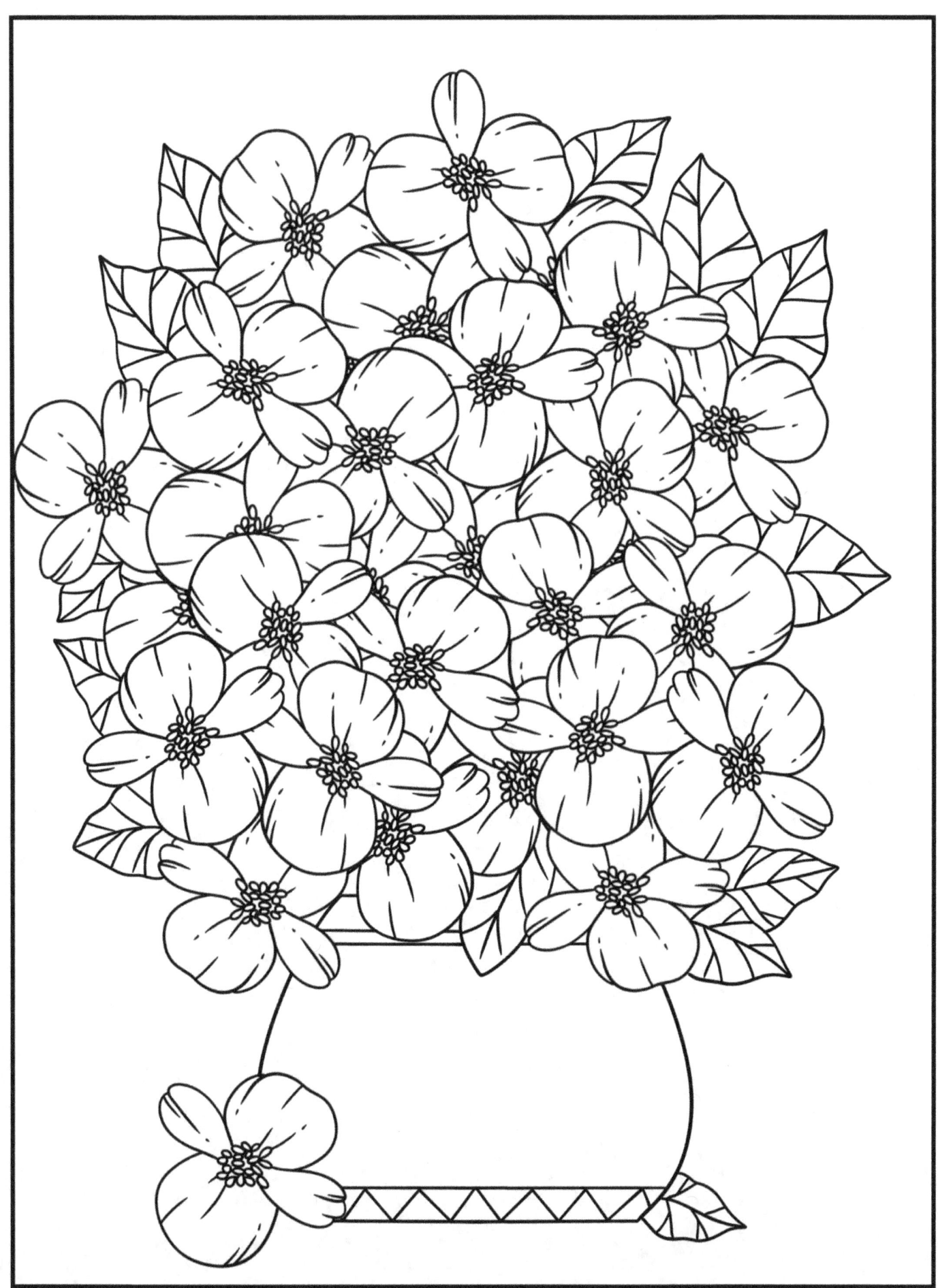

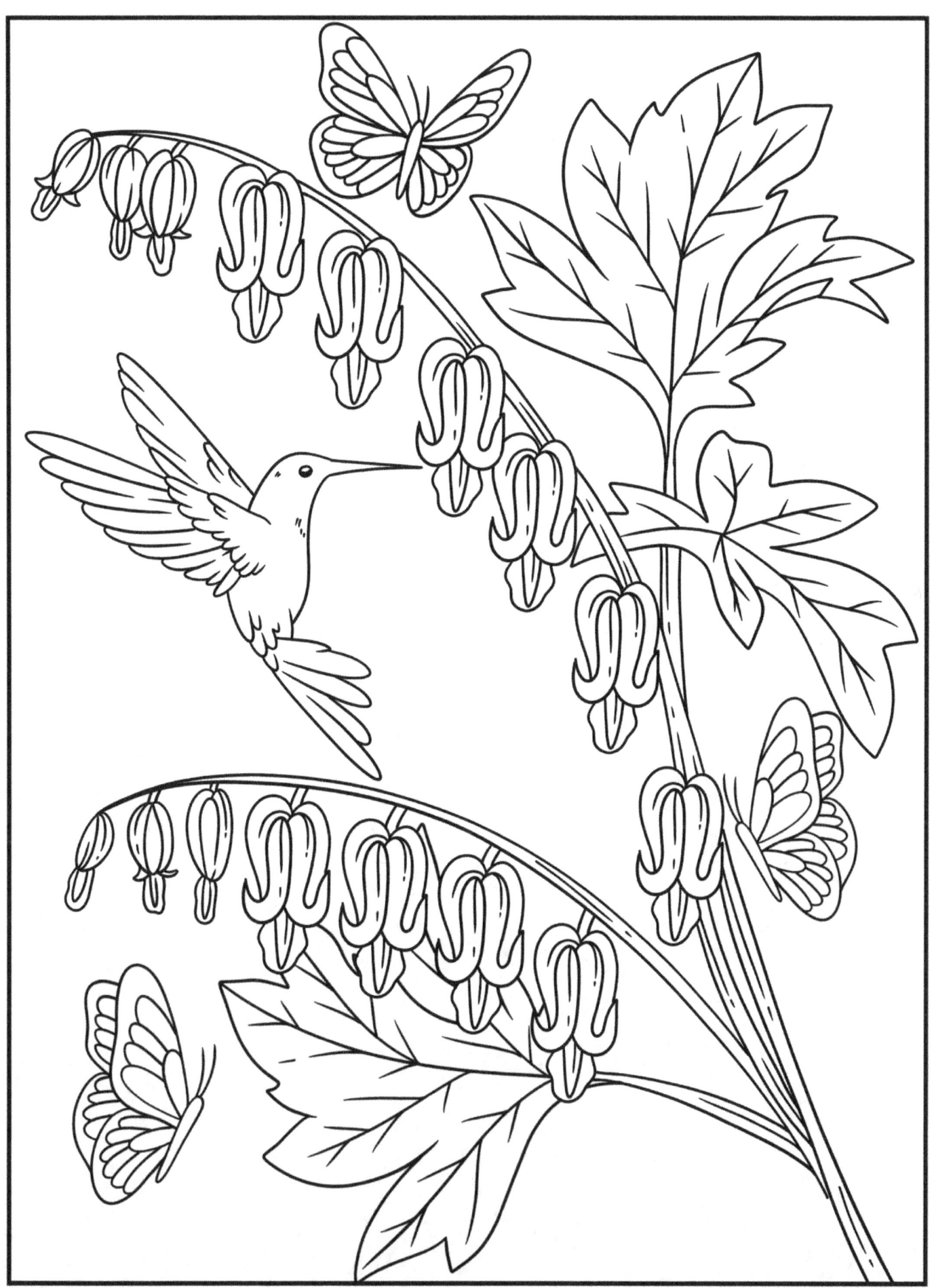

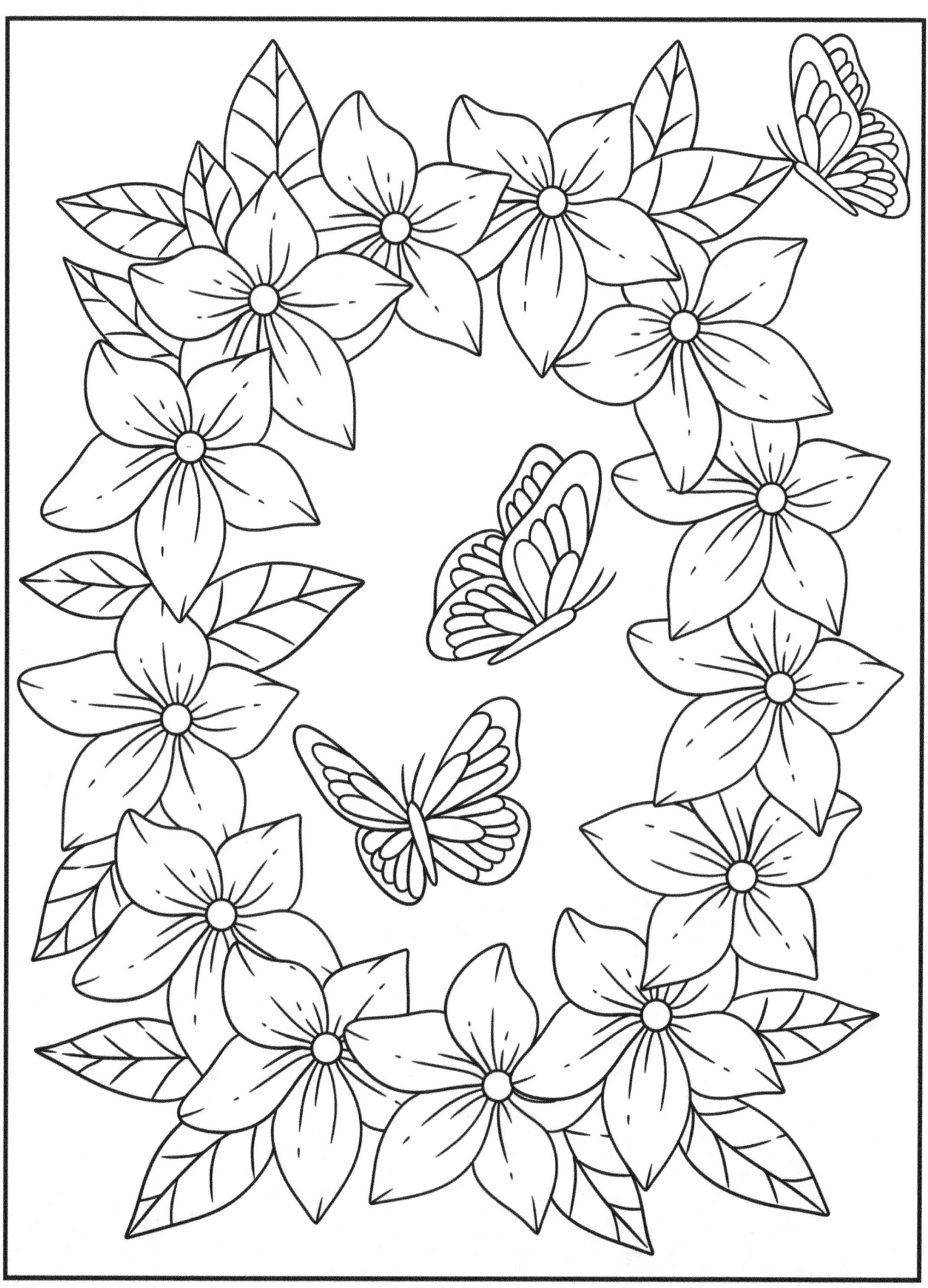

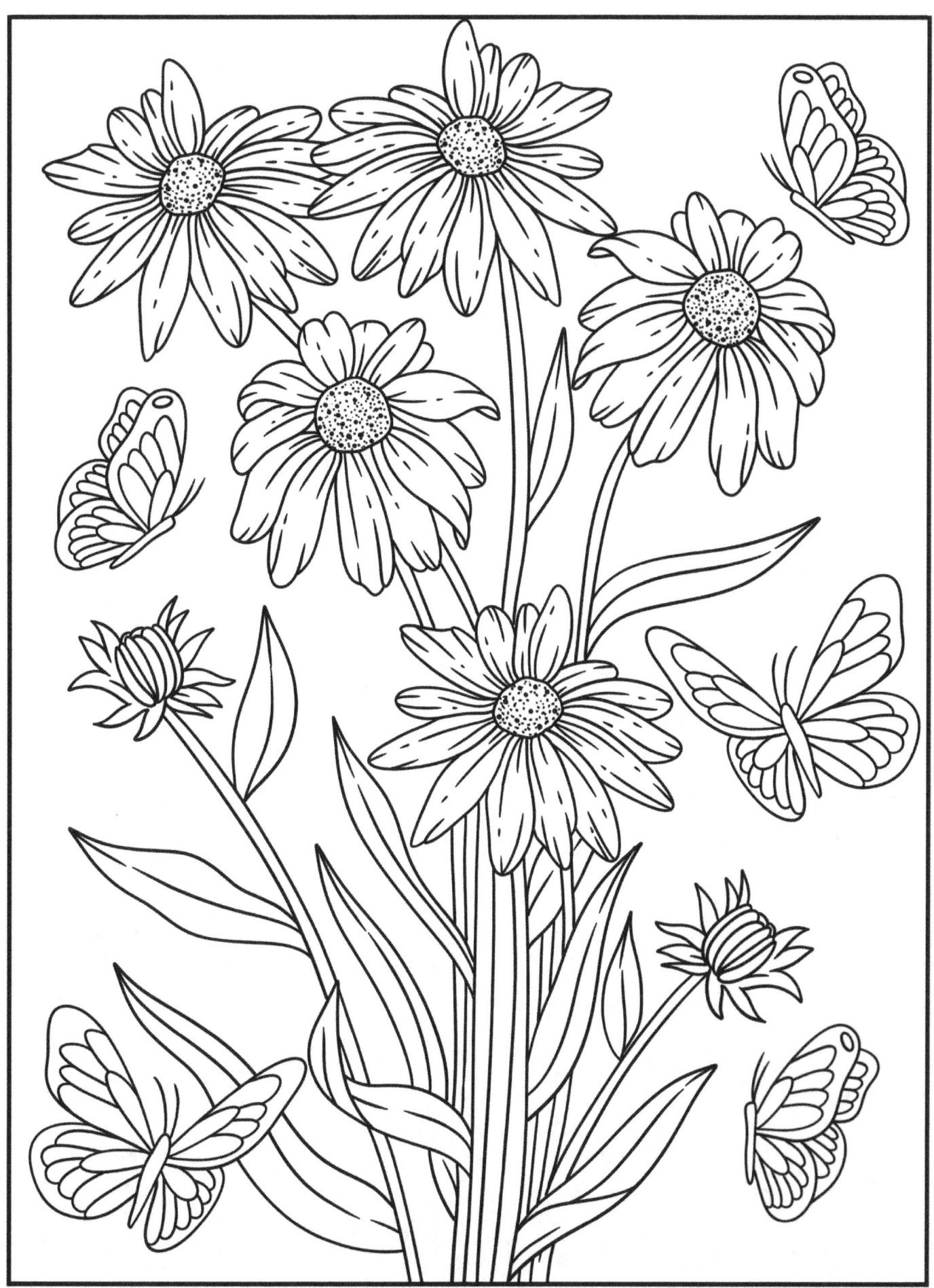

59

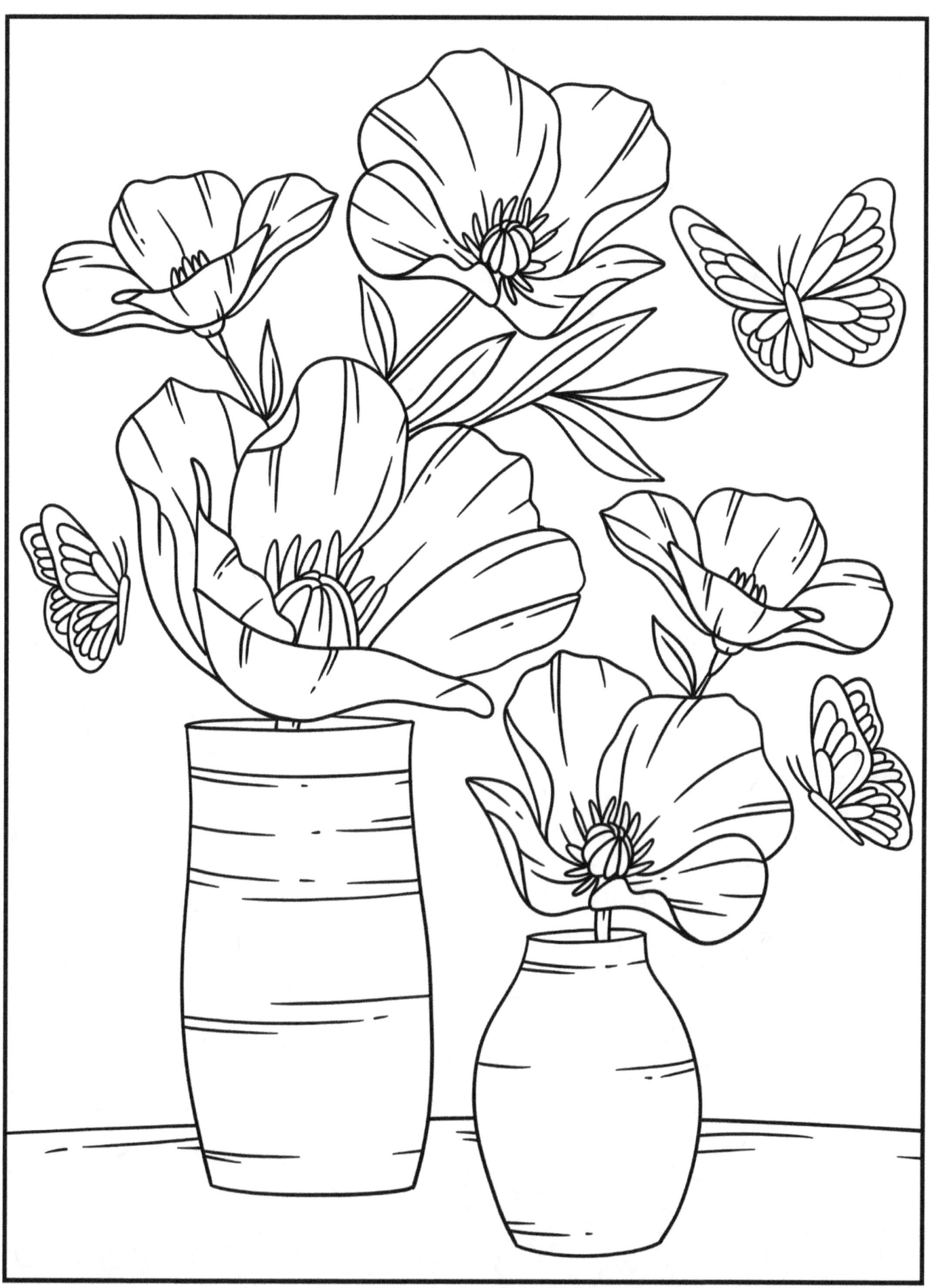

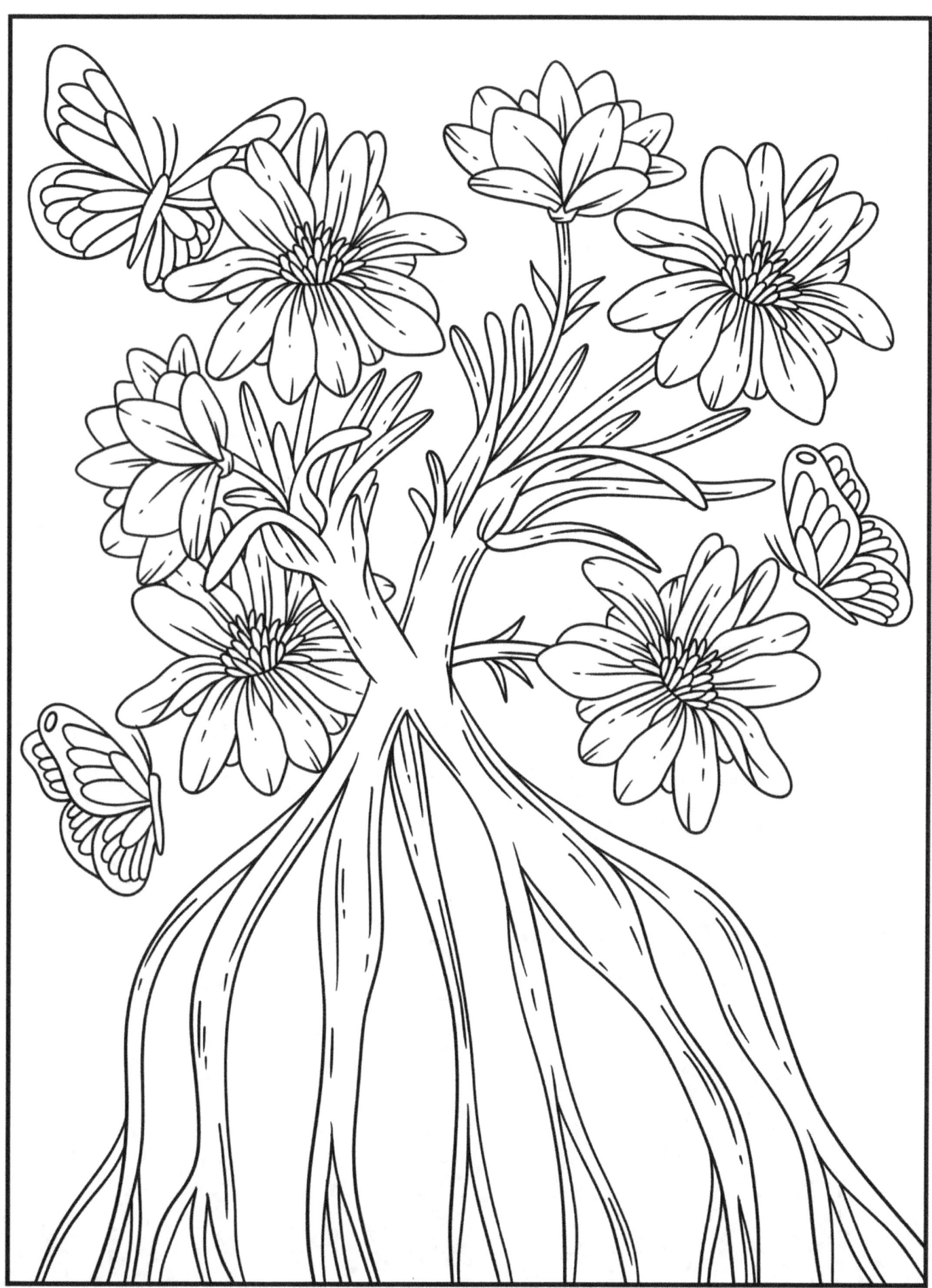

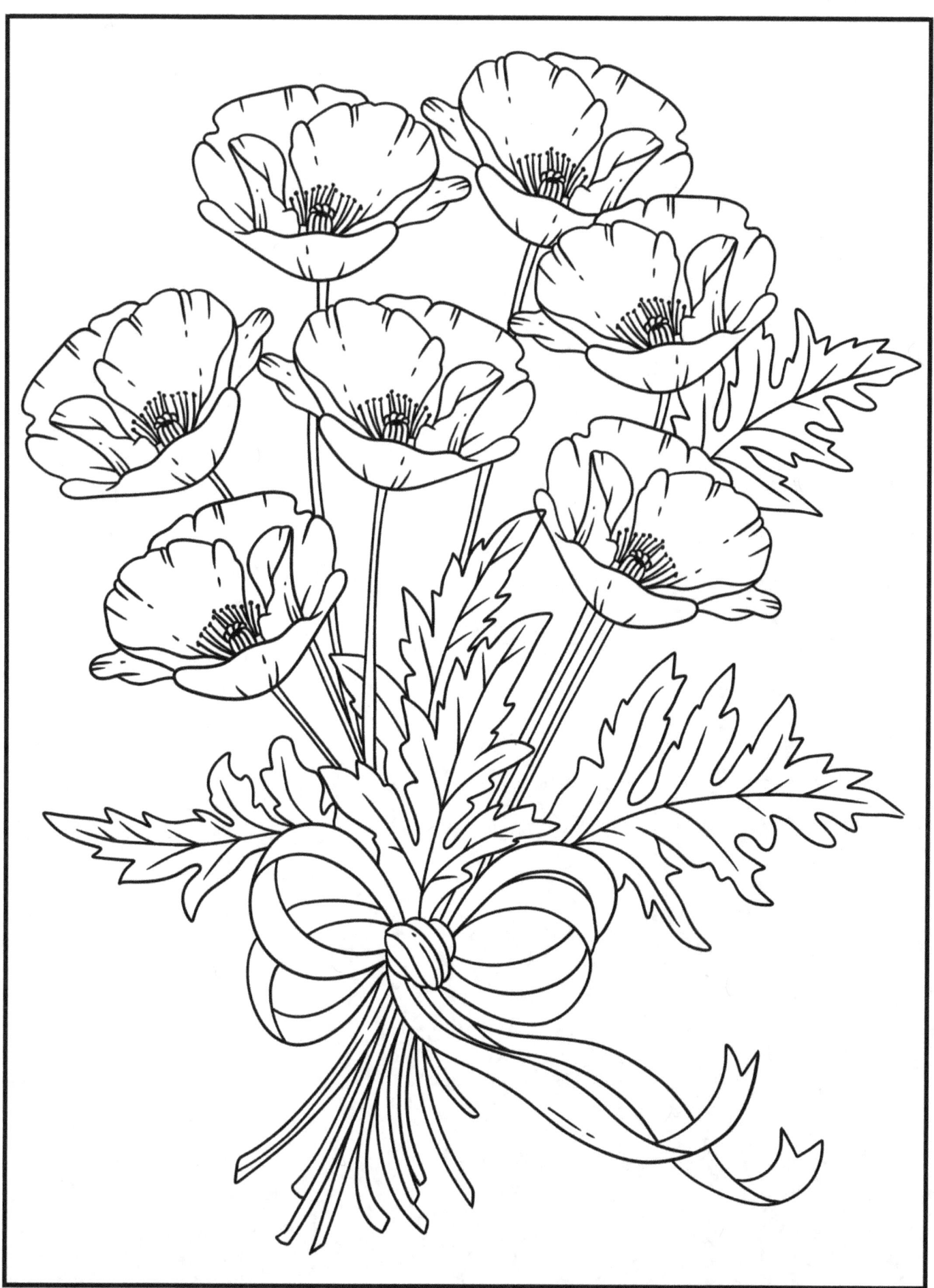

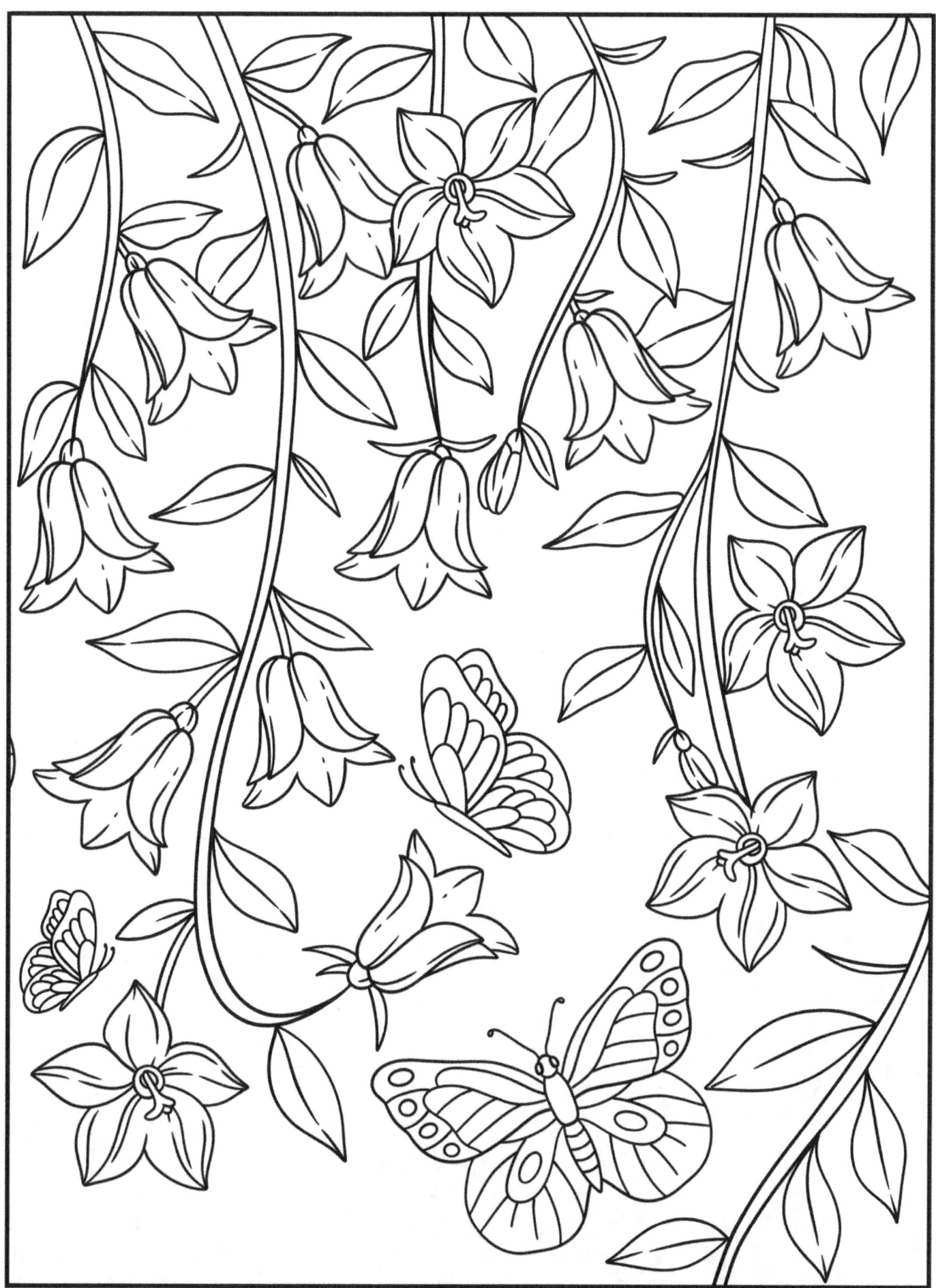

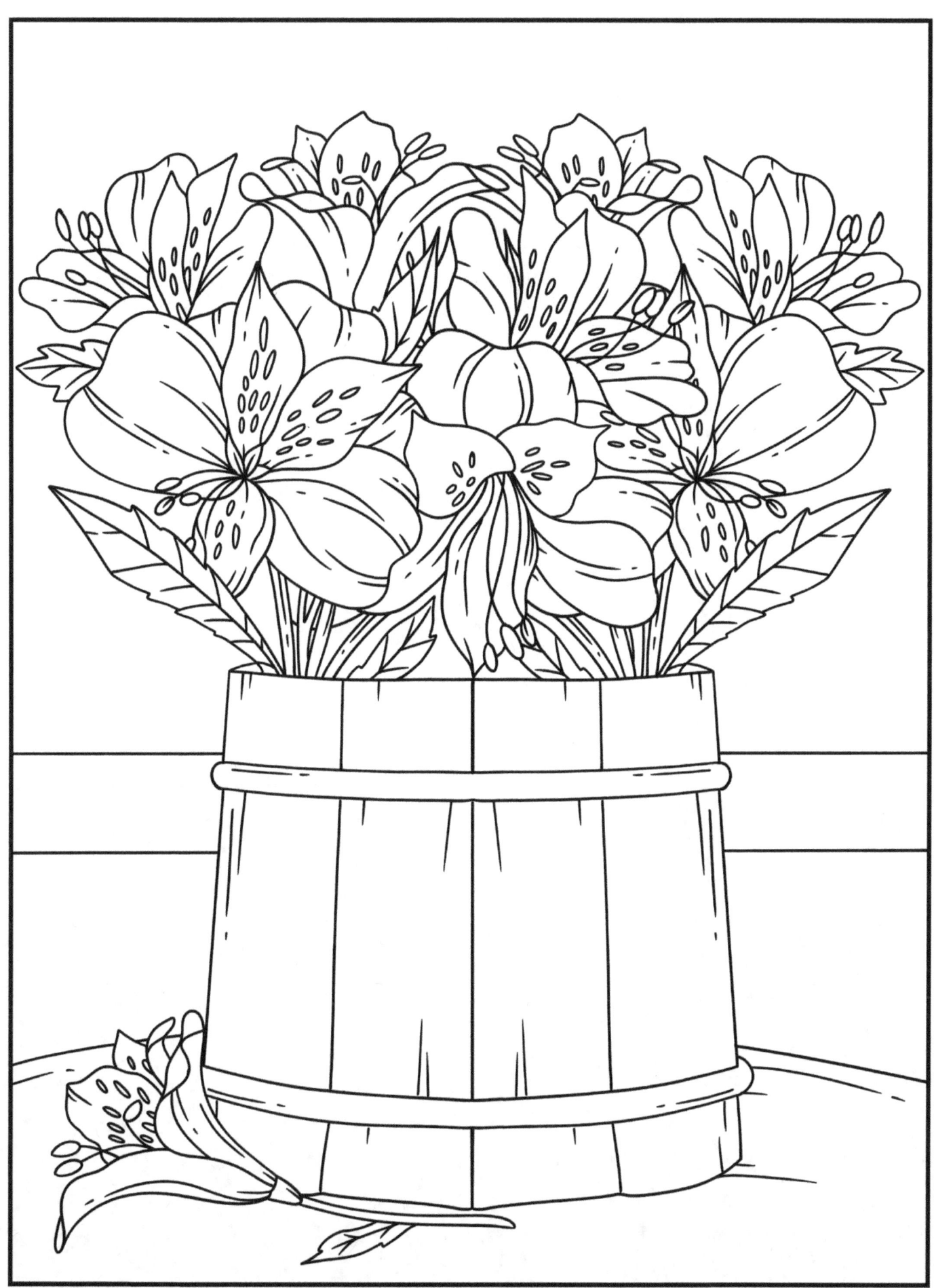

69

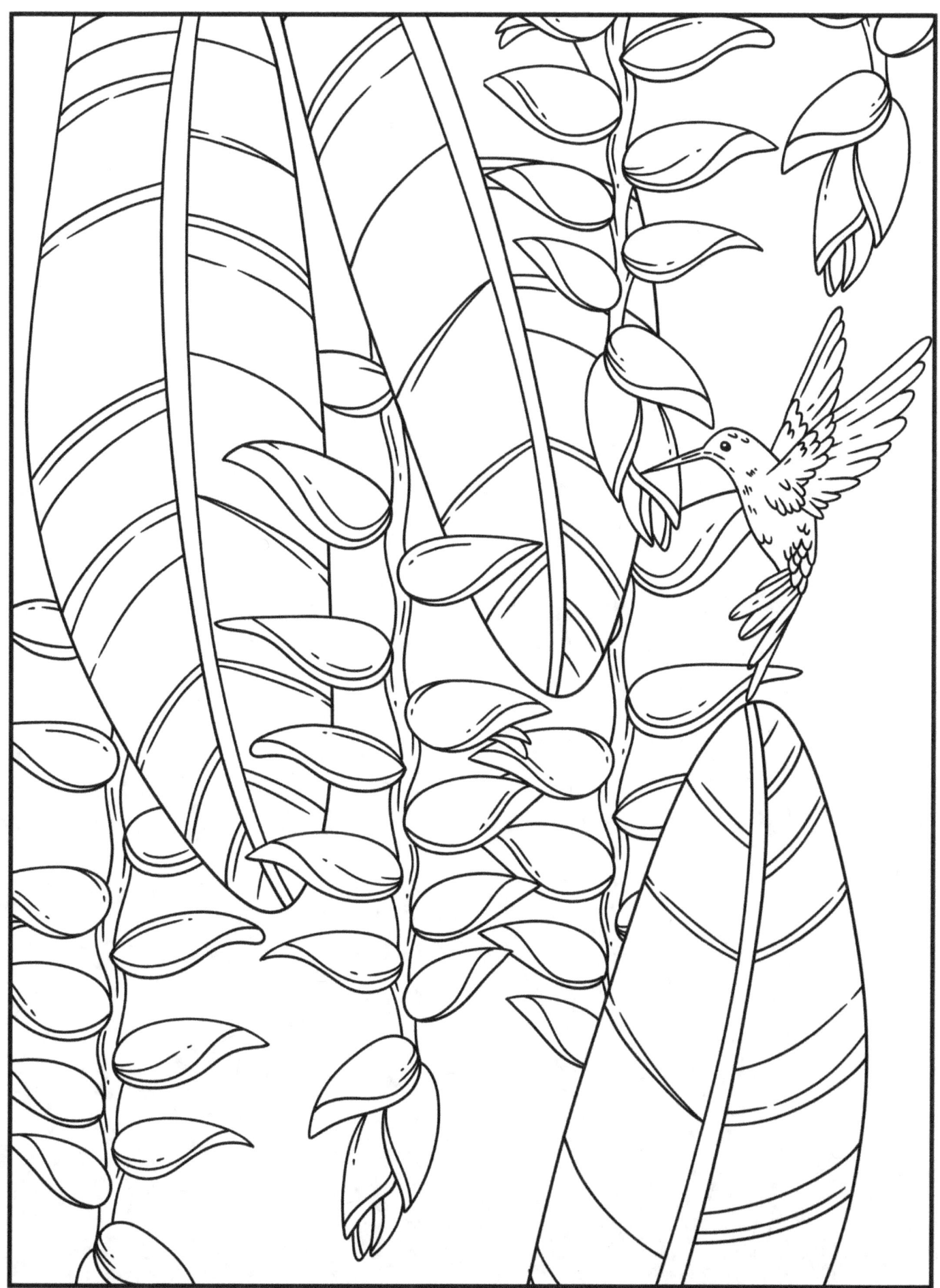

71

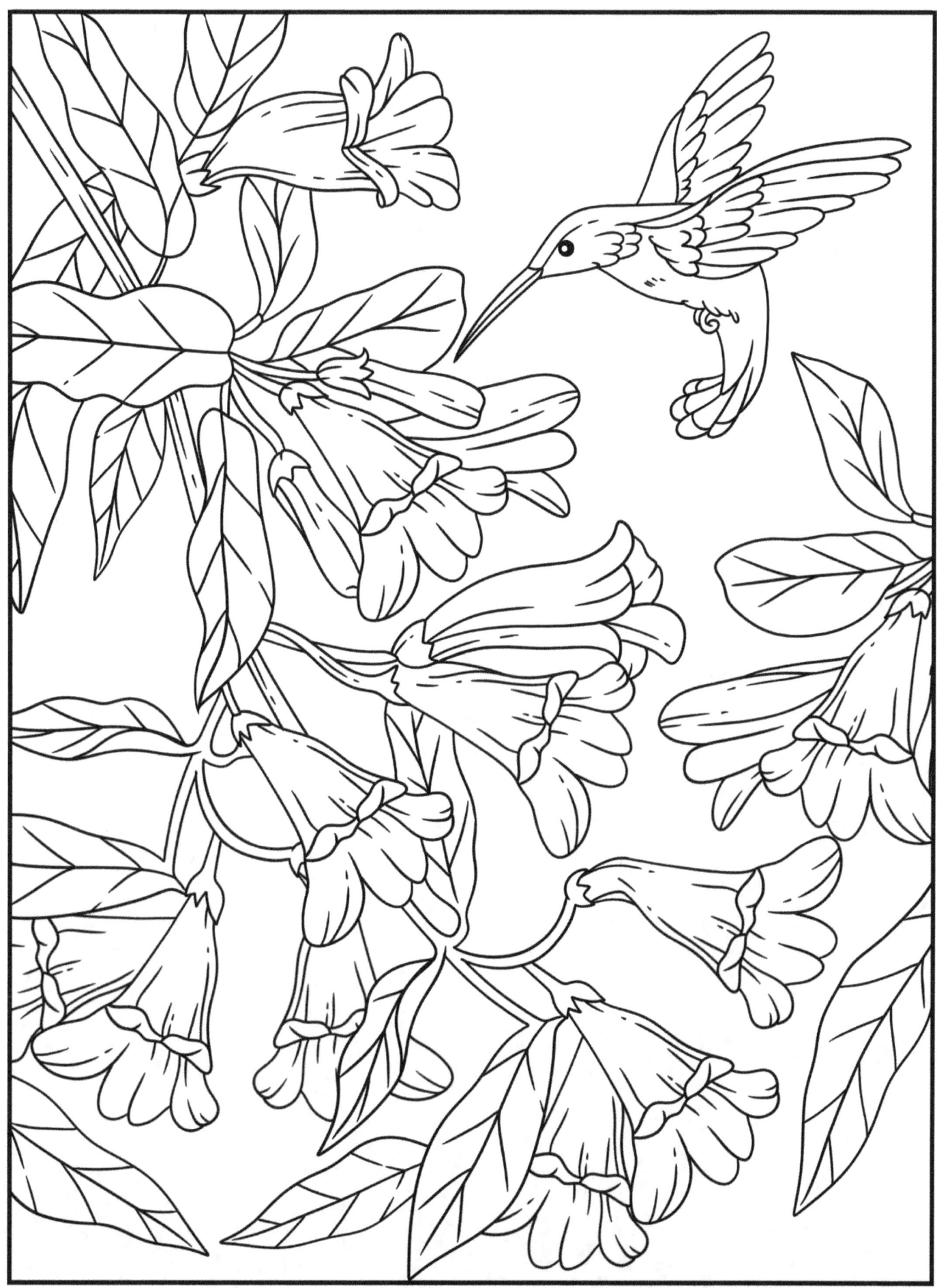

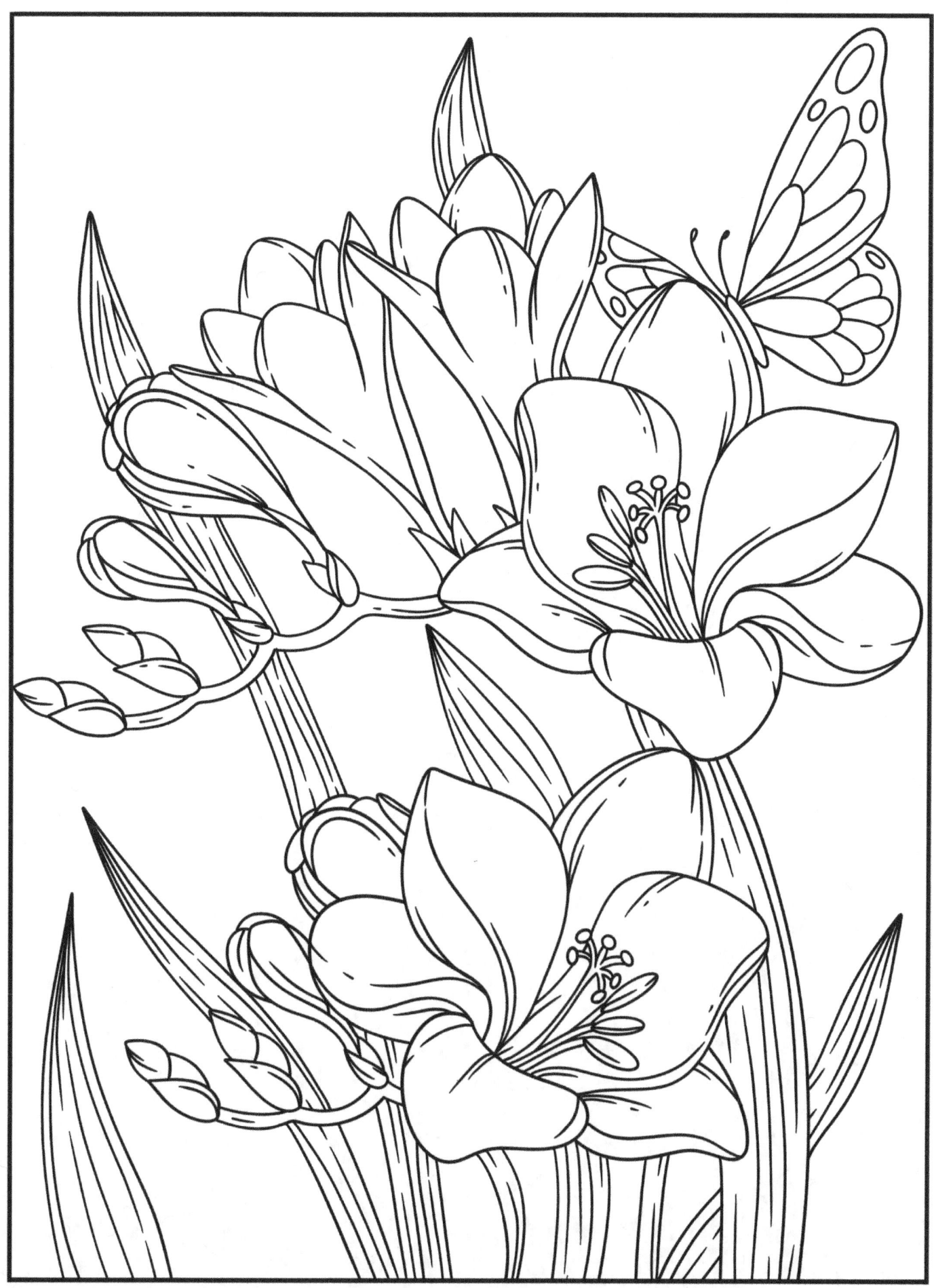

75

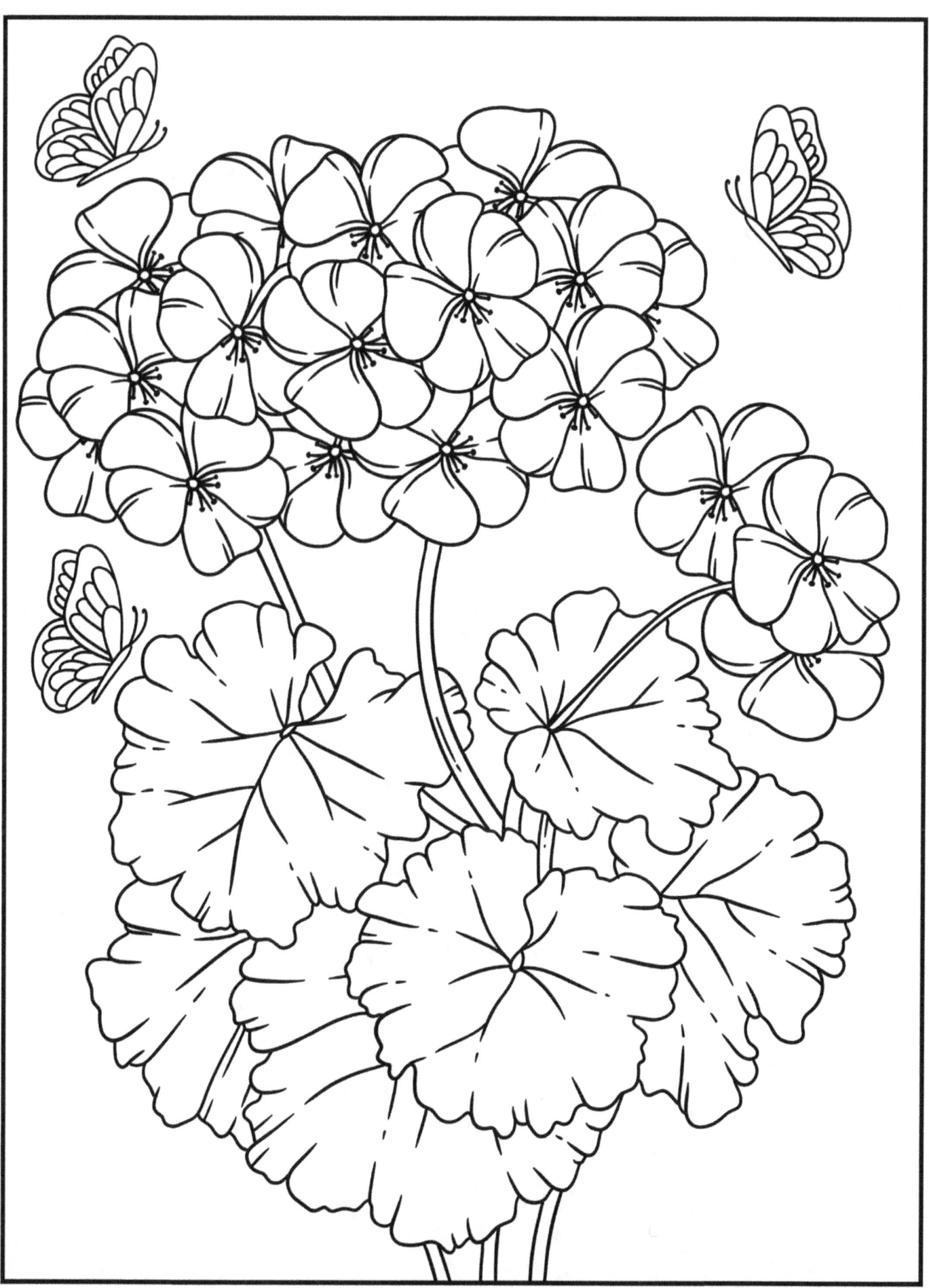

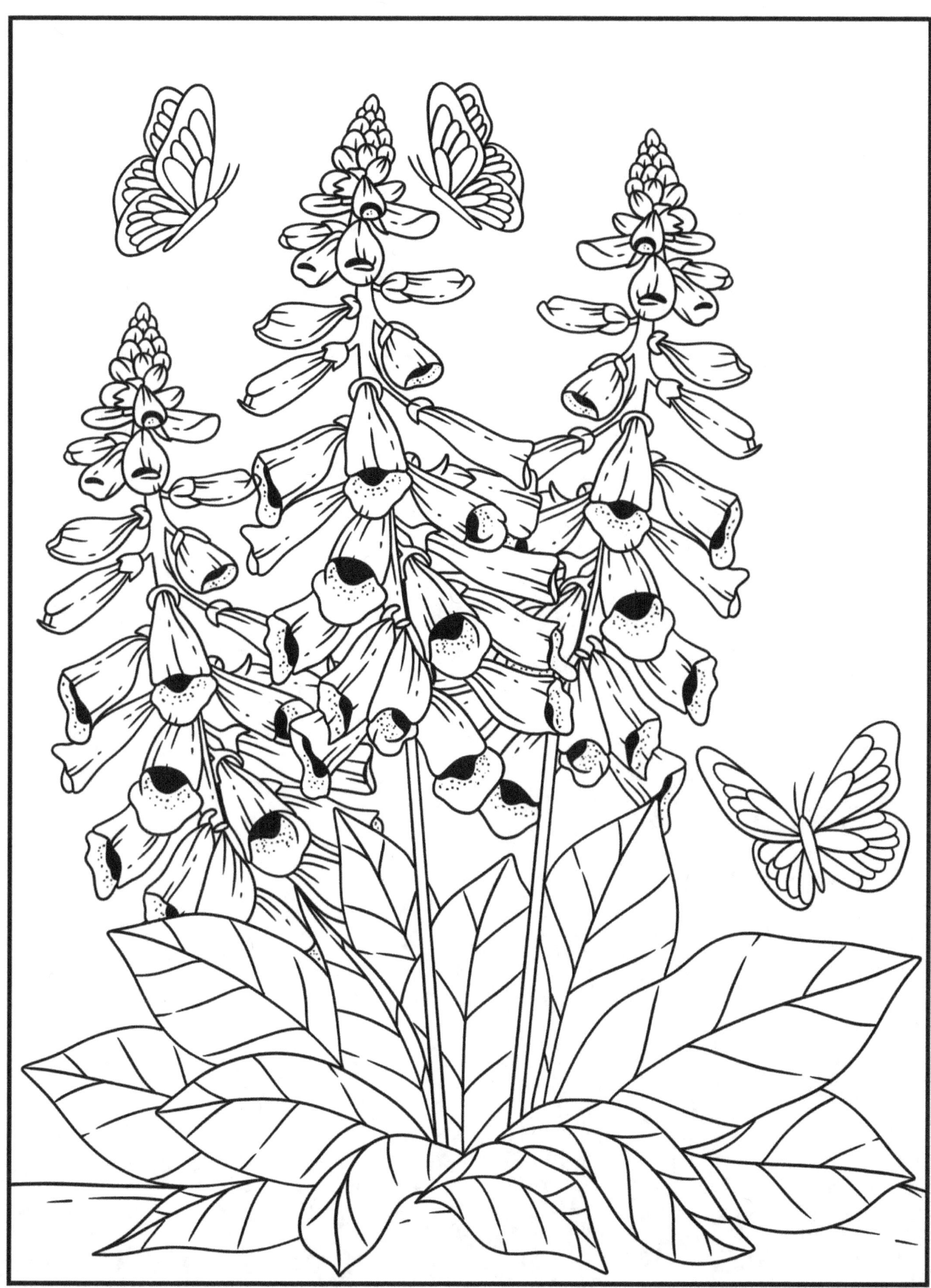

79

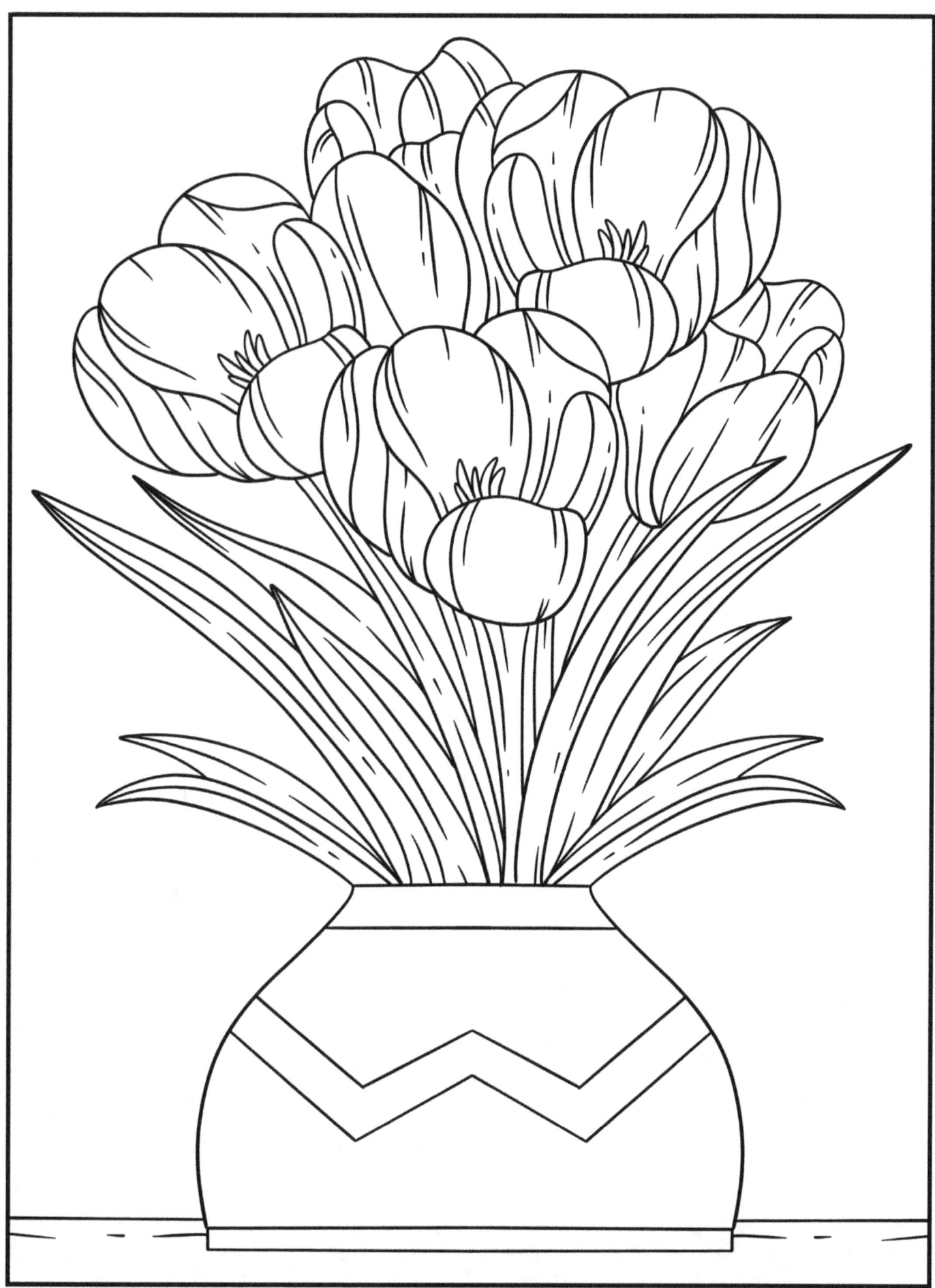

81

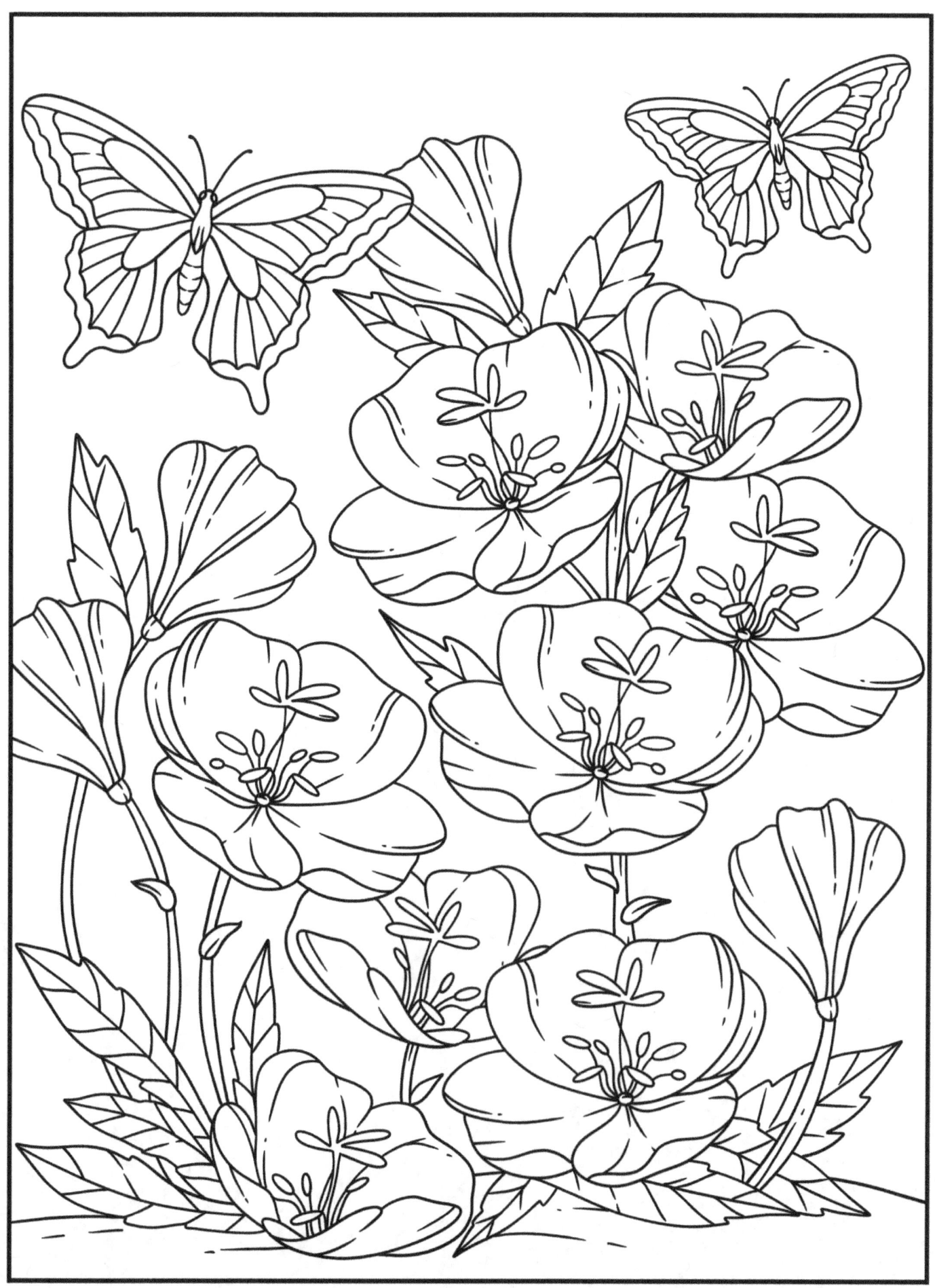

83

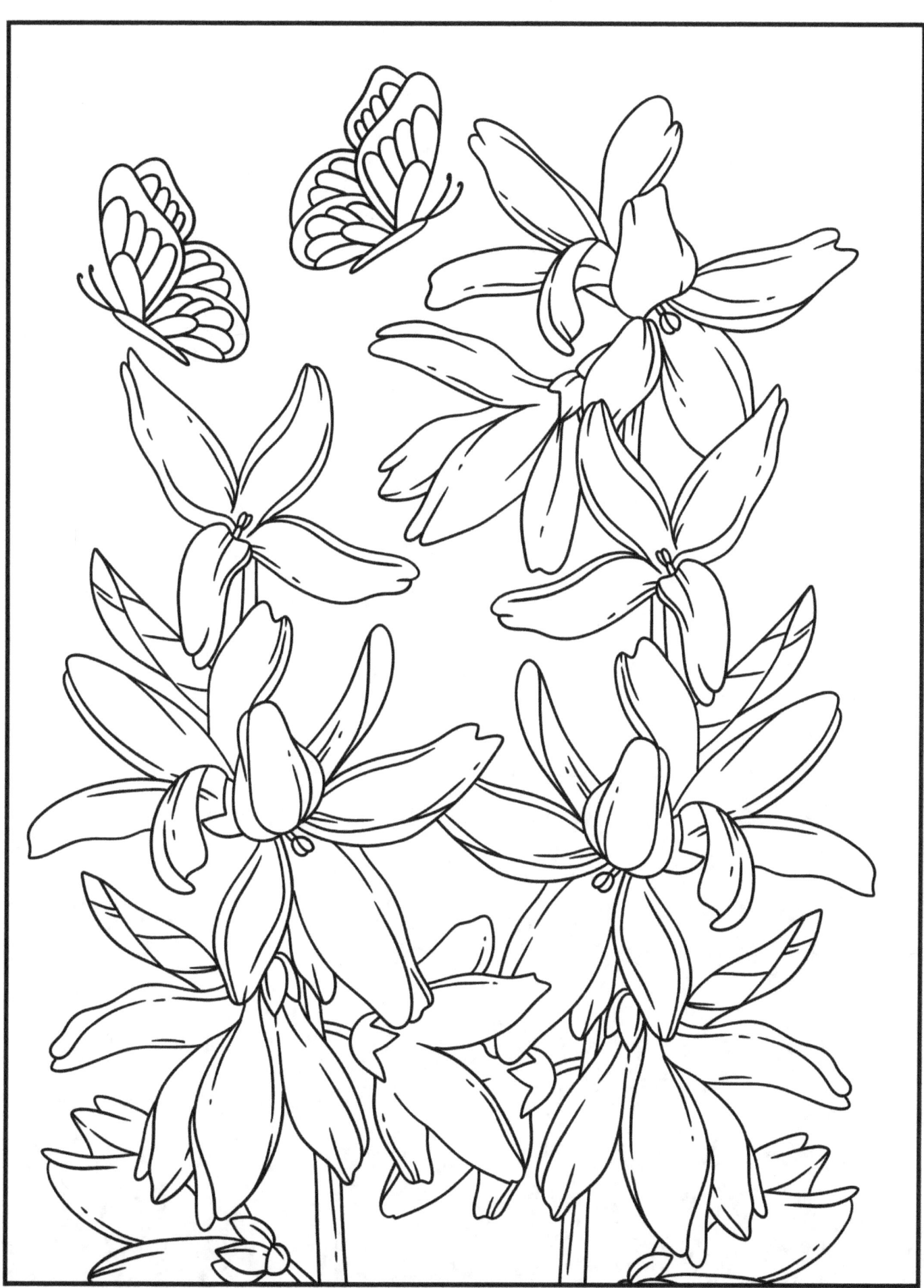

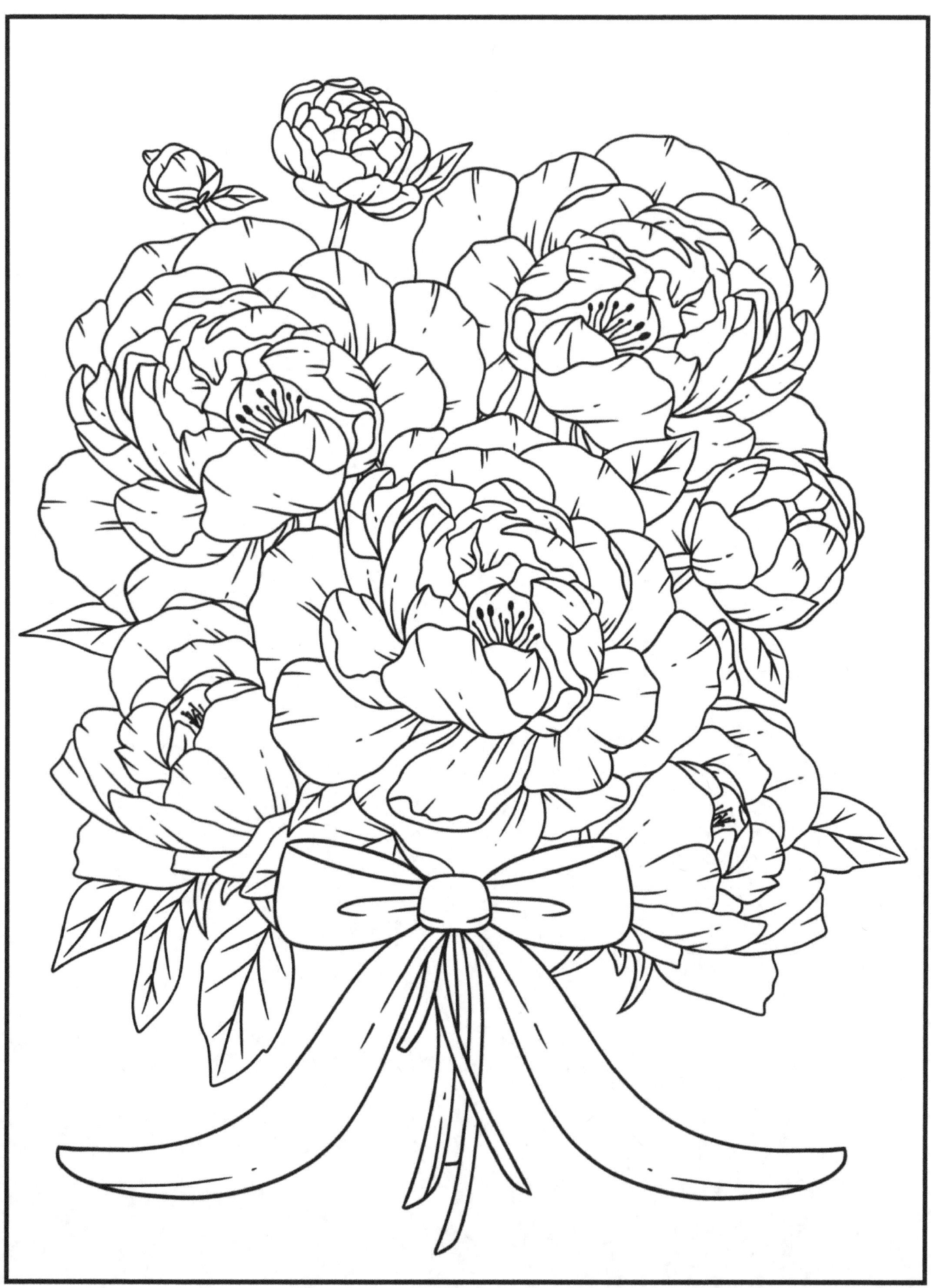

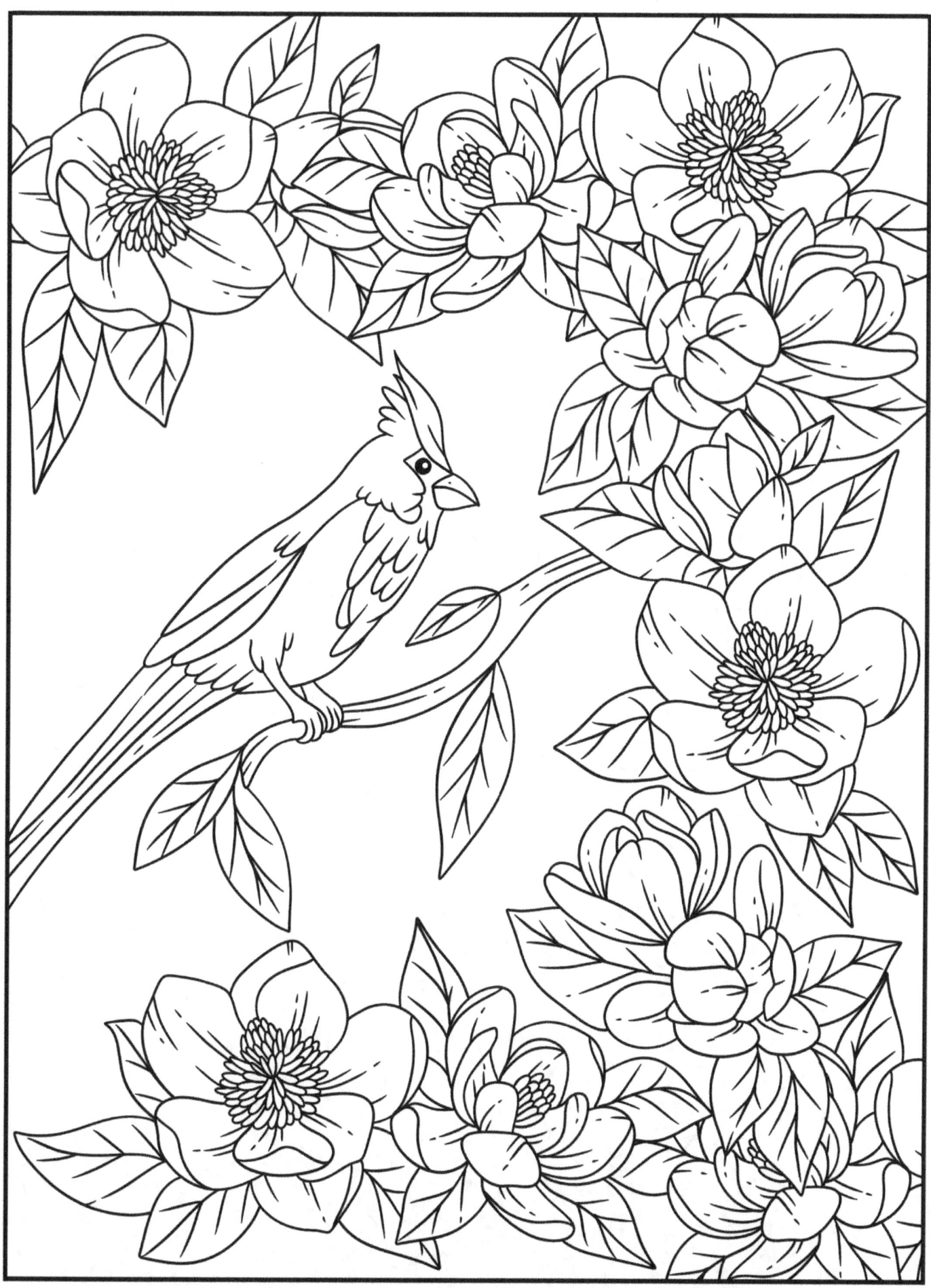

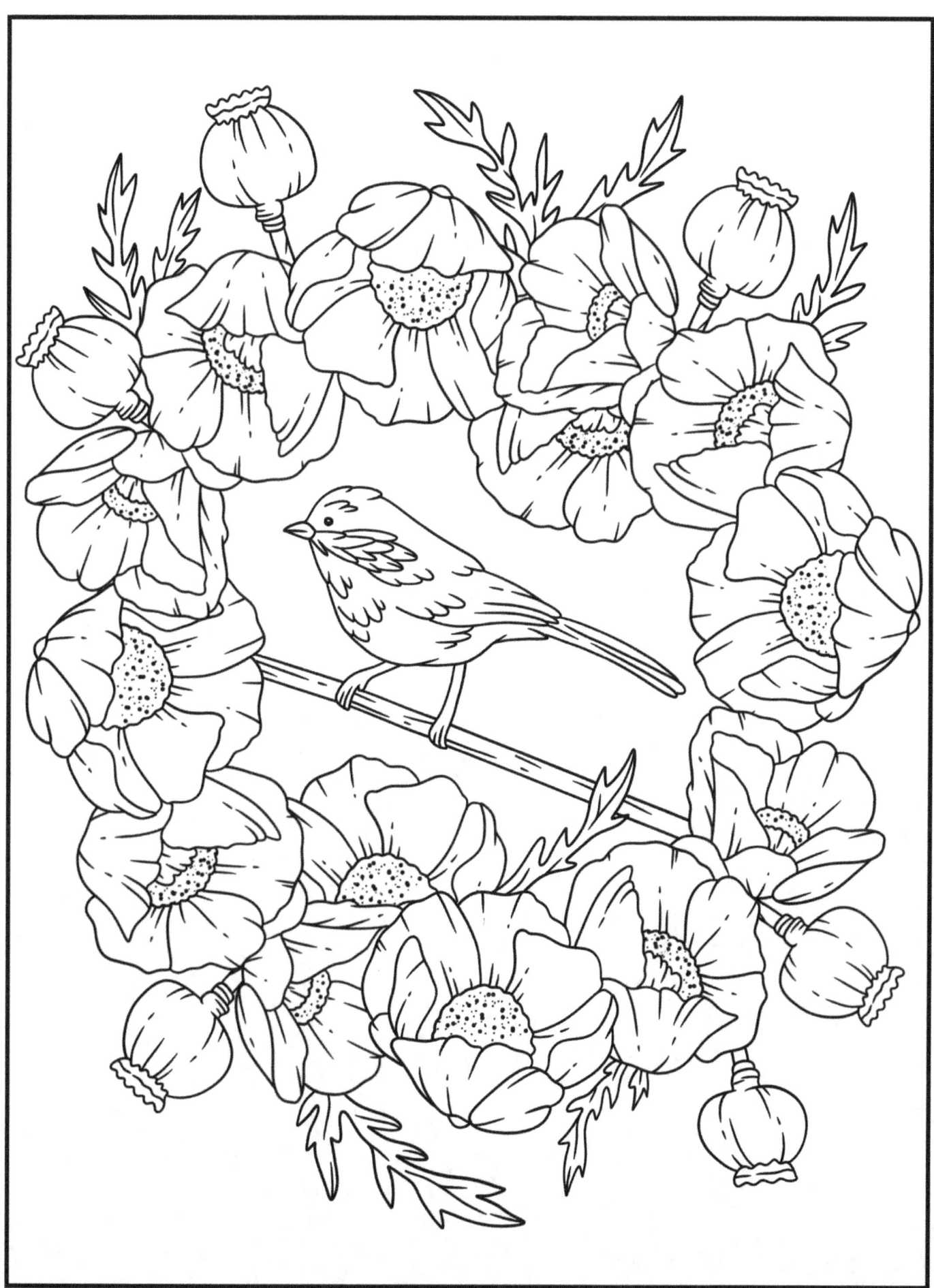

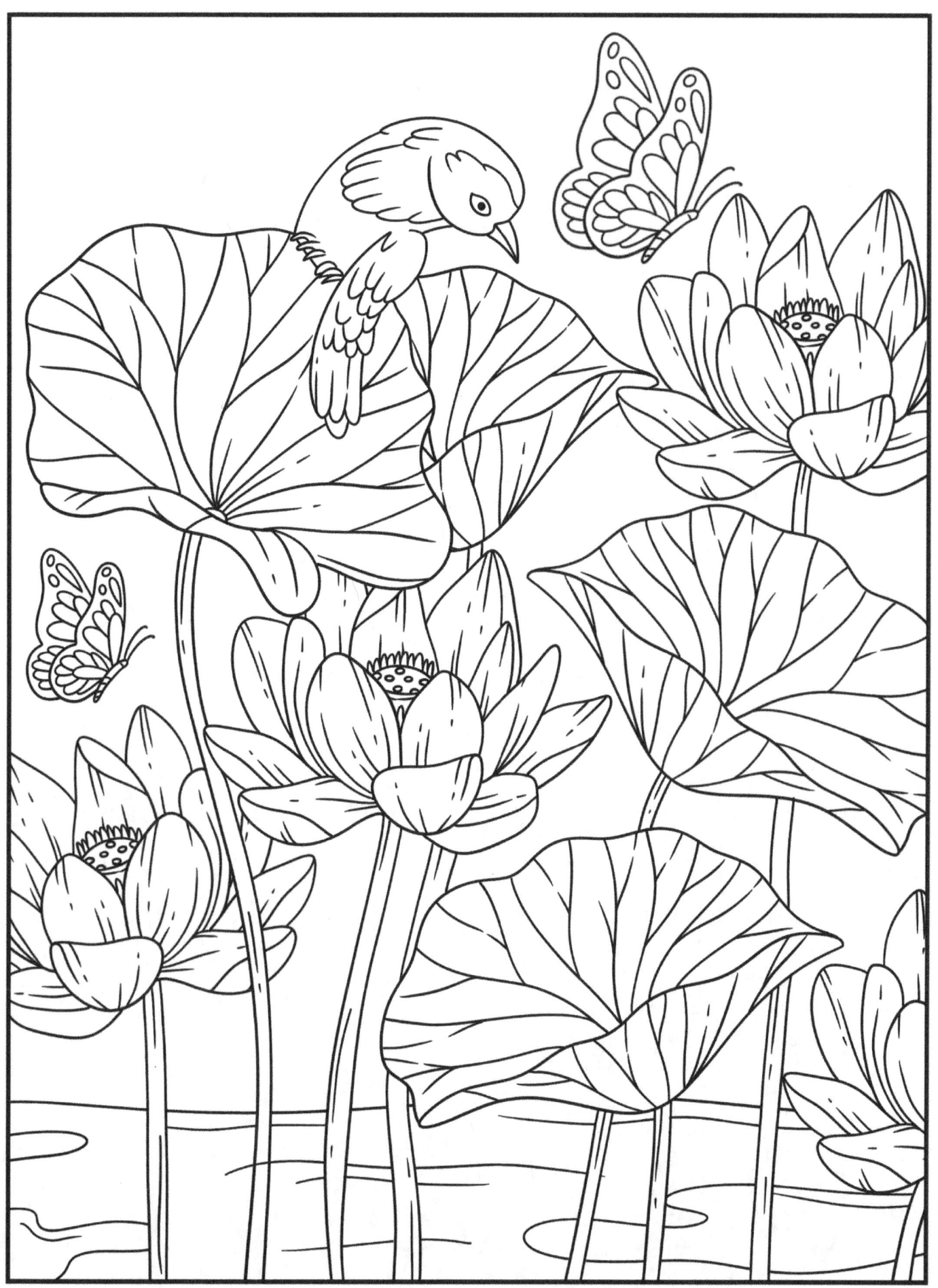

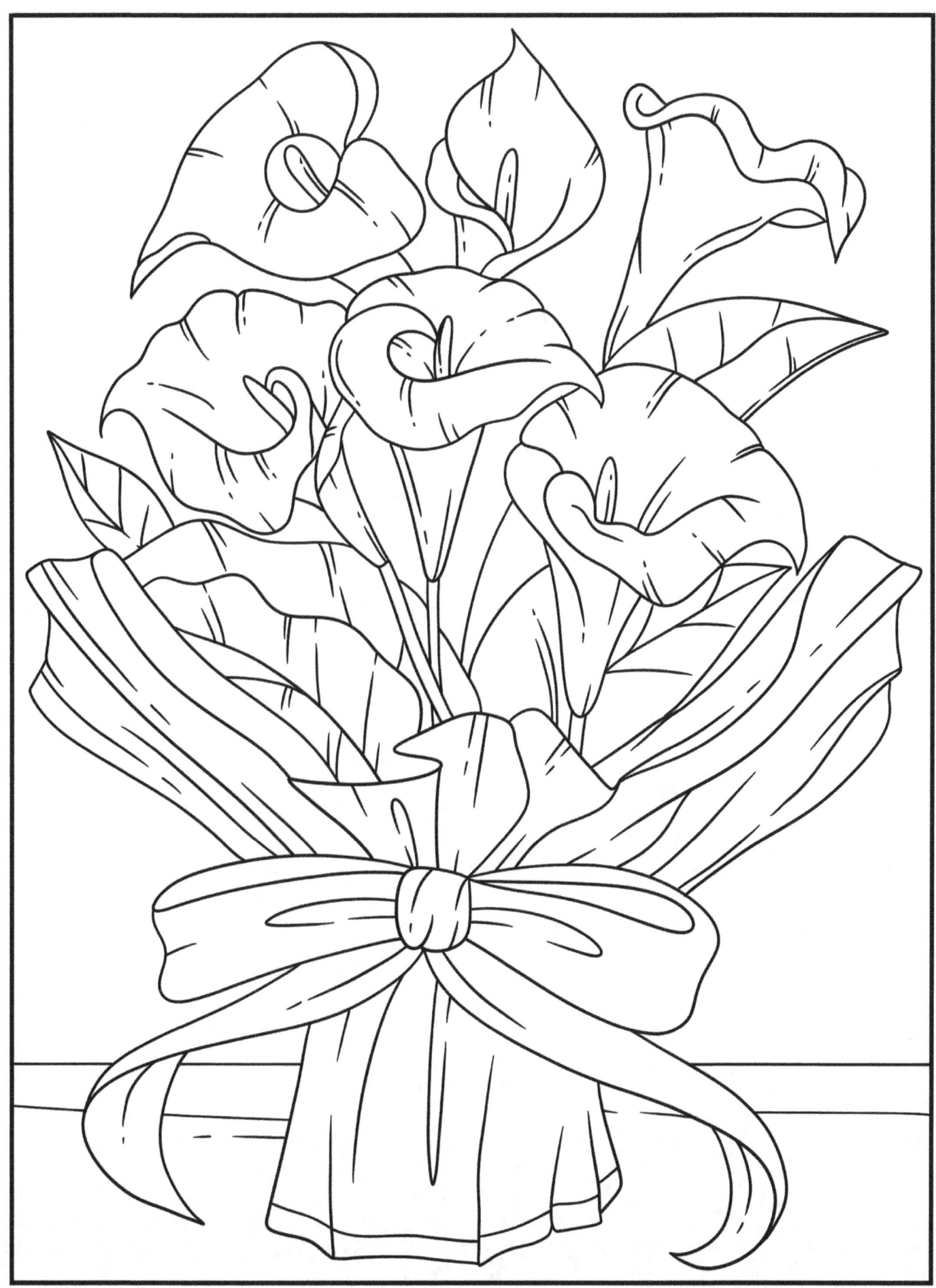

101

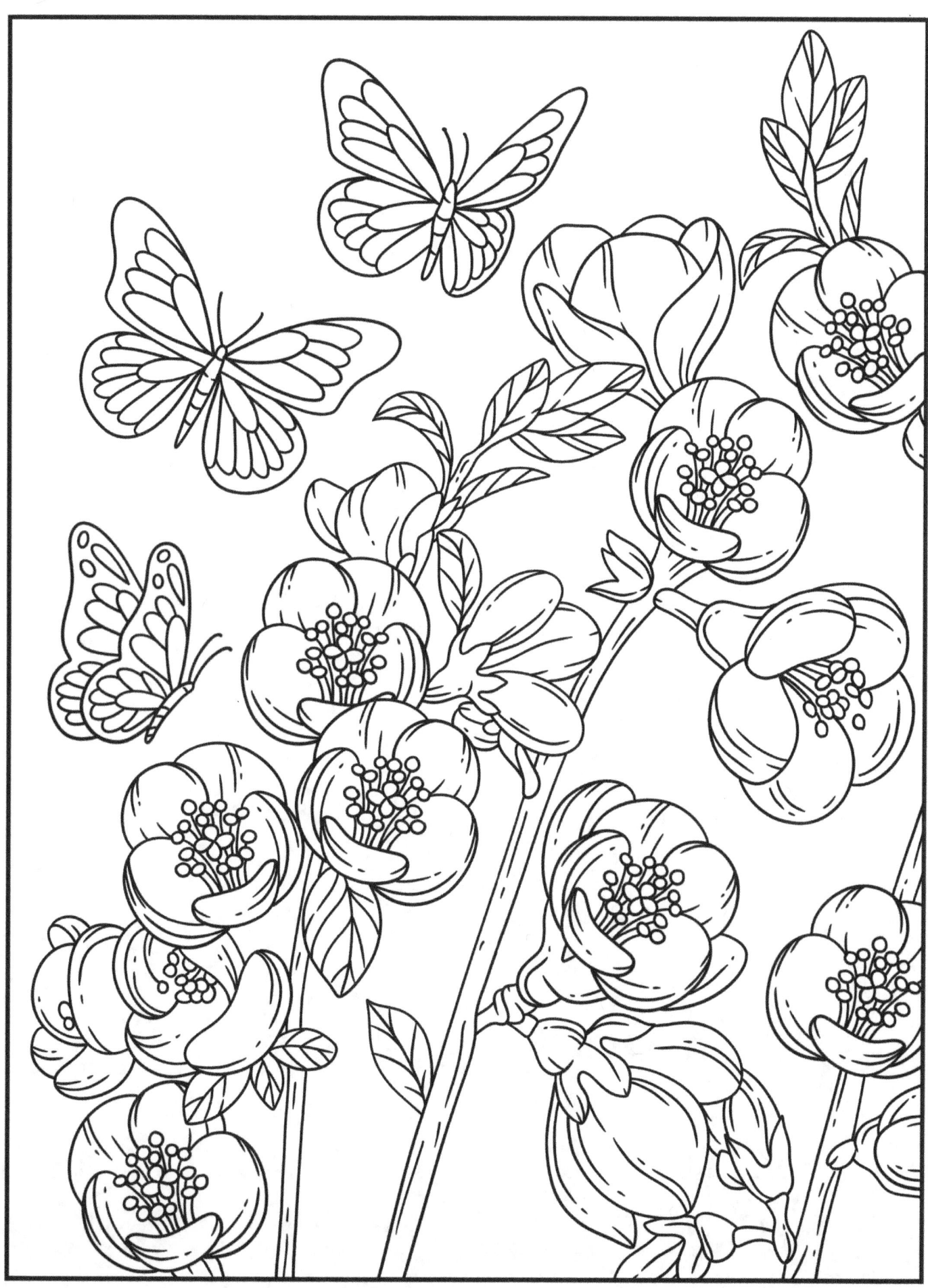

103

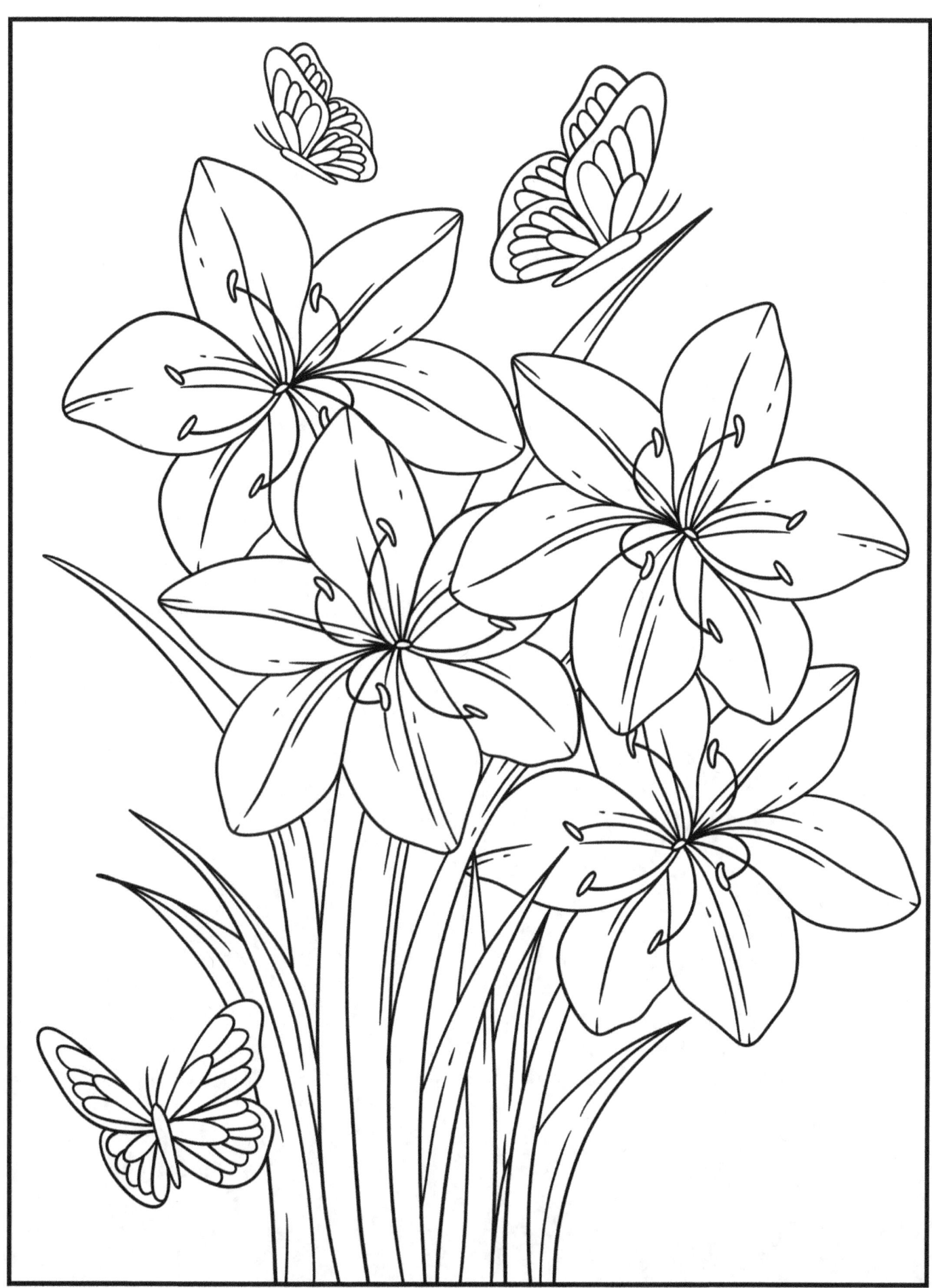

105

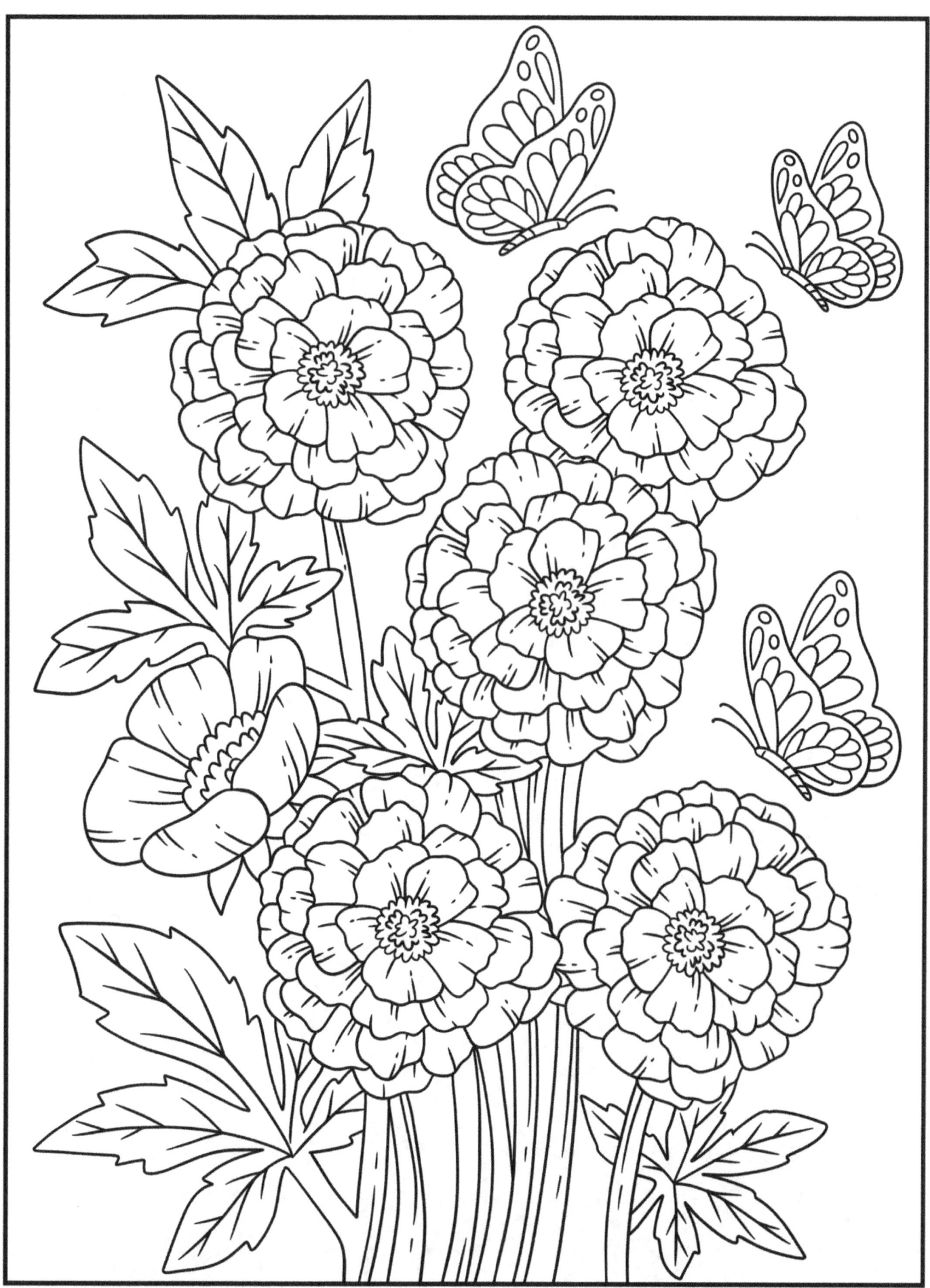